D0855604

MERLE ALLISON JOHNSON is pastor of First United Methodist Church in Forrest City, Arkansas. He has twenty-seven years of experience in average churches. Johnson is a prominent guest speaker and author of six previous books, including *Religious Roulette and Other Dangerous Games Christians Play* and *Sermons for Christian Seasons* for Abingdon.

HOW TO BE HAPPY
in The
non
ELECTRIC CHURCH

HOW TO BE HAPPY
in The
non
ELECTRIC CHURCH

Merle Allison Johnson

**ILLUSTRATED WITH LINE DRAWINGS
BY CHARLES COX**

Abingdon
Nashville

HOW TO BE HAPPY IN THE nonELECTRIC CHURCH

Copyright © 1979 by Abingdon

Library of Congress Cataloging in Publication Data

JOHNSON, MERLE ALLISON.
  How to be happy in the non-electric church.
  1. Small churches—Miscellanea. I. Title.
  BV637.8.J63   253   78-26463

ISBN 0-687-17706-5

Scripture quotations noted RSV are from the Revised
Standard Version of the Bible, copyrighted 1946, 1952, ©
1971, 1973.

MANUFACTURED BY THE PARTHENON PRESS AT
NASHVILLE, TENNESSEE, UNITED STATES OF AMERICA

For All the Saints in

Plumerville,
Worthington,
Mineral Springs,
Lake Village,
Malvern,
Eudora,
Siloam Springs, and
Forrest City

Contents

Preface

One of the most brutal revelations God ever gave to this, his servant, was when a "still small voice" whispered in my ear one day, "Merle, you are just barely a cut above average. If that!"

It took a while for me to accept this truth—about the same time it took for the Angel Moroni to get Joseph Smith's attention. But, pleasant or unpleasant, revelation is something I have in common with Joe, so I guess I've got as much right as he had to share it.

My credentials for being ordinary are excellent, and I'm not embarrassed to say so. After all, no one is likely to bother to dispute this claim. So, in view of my credentials to do so, I am writing this little book for Christians just a cut above average, in churches of the same level. If that!

The delusion that I was above average started during World War II when I was in the seventh grade. That year was just one of many wonderful ones I spent in an idyllic little town called Cotton Plant. One day Miss Sue Anna Yarbrough, the prettiest seventh-grade teacher in the South, told our class that America was the land of equal opportunity. She told us it was possible that one of us young boys would be President of the United States. We had to dream big dreams, she said. Now, that got my attention.

Miss Sue Anna and I had a secret, although we never talked about it. *I was to be President of the United States.* I knew she had been talking about me that day. So I kept this cherished secret for a long time. In fact, if there are one or two more Watergate-like scandals up on the hill, I may still be draftable!

Yet, at some point I gave up any real notion of gaining the presidency; I studied for the Christian ministry instead,

9

transferring my sights to a position of comparable prestige—pastor of Riverside Church in New York. But then I drove through New York during the rush hour some ten years ago. That became one of the most moving spiritual experiences I ever had. I was never out of contact with God for one second! I laid it all on the altar right then and there! I confessed my vain desires and turned Riverside Church over to Ernest Campbell.

However, I was not cured. My delusion of superiority continued to surface for years, in many ways. My members would tell me I was "going someplace." Now "someplace" (sometimes reduced to "places") is a term people use when they think you might leave the locals and go higher. That day finally came.

I now have arrived. I'm in Forrest City. The Moroni-like voice in my ear has whispered that I am *at* it. I can stop waiting for the big break. I am lucky to be where I am. Well, so what? I wouldn't know what to do anywhere else. My credentials fit me only for a degree of beautiful mediocrity. I can handle that. Ours is an average church. I know that, because our attendance is running less than it did last year! In that sense, this is not a book by a "successful" pastor!

I awoke one morning to the fact that I have a daughter in Ole Miss, and another who is a high school senior. I am like thousands of other midforty folks with girls in school—broke. ("Liquid assets" is a term which was coined for this time in life. Every penny is on the run.) In fact, every time I try to figure out where I am, on a scale from A to F, I keep coming back to middle C. I have written several books. That's above average. One was a bomb, one did pretty well, the others were so-so. Give me a B and a D. That equals C.

I nearly hyperventilated when the bookstore representative held up my books at my annual conference. That's above average. I felt a sickness unto death when they sold them for 25¢ in the "junk" display the next year. (Talk about a bunch of nauseating two-bit jokes.) That's another D, maybe an F. It doesn't matter. It all adds up to a finely tuned degree of mediocrity. Even my timing has always been bad. I wrote *How to Murder a Minister,* and they promptly did away with the death penalty. I wrote *Beyond*

Disenchantment, and no one cared to ask why. By the time *The Kingdom Seekers* came out, everyone had quit seeking. I then was led like a lamb to that bookstore slaughter sale, where all my friends who had purchased my books at the list price demanded a refund. But at least I'm not a coward. I managed to walk through those nine people with steady nerves and an "overcoming the world" smile.

I've had eight churches, including student appointments, over the last twenty-seven years. My entire experience has been in average churches, with just average people. And that's good. *I* think it is. And I think somebody needs to say a good word for all those good folks and all those corner-lot churches. It is said that they are a vanishing breed—that, like the boll-weevil, they're just looking for a home.

Wrong! We are *not* dead yet. And we *have* a home. In fact, I would say that the local vanilla church is "alive and well." (I'm sick of that overworked phrase. The first time I saw it, it was applied to Satan, who certainly gets enough press these days.) To be more exact, the local church is not really well, but we are alive. In spite of statistics which indicate that we are losing out, we are on the rise because of some newfound reasons for our existence. Actually, some of these reasons are just up-to-date reaffirmation of the old ones. This is an upbeat book. It is not meant to be irreverent, but by all that's right, it *is* intended to be frank and candid. I am writing for you, if you're interested in the local church, nonElectric variety. You can tune in most anyplace and find we are on common ground. I *am* addressing *both laity and the clergy.* Also, I want us all to do some thinking about being small! This book might be called, *How to Think Small Wholesomely.* I want to give you some ideas about attitudes and methods that work for the average local church, the church that will never be electrifying!

Actually, my suggestions are for churches of *all* sizes. That is, for those that are struggling to maintain their identity. The Electric Church is imposing its model on local churches as never before.

What is the Electric Church? It is usually that stage area before the camera—*nothing more*—and, when compared to the local church—*much less!* Local churches that telecast and broadcast are *not* included in my definition of Electric. (That is, unless they use this means to collect money in order to compete with struggling local churches.) The time-honored use of the media by local churches is for the purpose of ministry, and *no solicitation of funds is employed.*

Therefore, I am a very average parish pastor, who is more than a little concerned that we see the situation for what it is. I am speaking for thousands of common pastors who are becoming aware of a startling truth. *The Electric Church may not be our friend!*

Finally, I know I am average for another excellent reason. I can remember when my people would say. "We don't know how long we can keep you," or, "We know we are bound to lose you soon, and it worries us." They don't say that anymore. In fact, the last furrowed brow I saw in this church was when the lead soprano asked me if I had anything for a sinus headache.

My personal secretary, Virginia Buck, has my deepest gratitude for working with almost illegible script. I am grateful to Nan Montgomery, our church secretary, for her assistance in proofreading. It will be worth it, if a few people who love local churches can use some of these ideas.

—Merle Allison Johnson

1

Most of God's Children
Can Qualify
for nonElectric Status

Now that I have given my best shot at establishing my credentials in mediocrity, I want to suggest subject matter that may have been a concern of yours, whether you are of the clergy or the laity. Do you feel the way I feel? Much of this material has to do with Christianity's Electric World. Let us take a look.

1. Will you acknowledge that you can't quite fathom why the world's best-known faith healer is building the world's best medical facility?

2. Do you wonder why there were not "helpful" drawings in Marabel Morgan's book?

3. Will you admit that you are more than a little puzzled by what Ruth, Larry, and Chaplain Bob have in common?

4. Despite tending to agree with Anita on the gay thing, do you wonder how she is getting more mileage out of this than Moses got from his Red Sea drama?

5. Will you join me in encouraging a National Gabriel Awards night, so we all can see whose darling wife will win best supporting actress?

6. Do you wonder why God keeps confusing us by raising up so many great voices, each claiming to be "the one for our times"?

7. Have you wondered why most of the religious media stars have ceased using props which made the studio look like the average church sanctuary?

8. Have you wondered how some of these people can live down scandals that would do in a local pastor?

9. Have you noticed that being born again means you no longer have any privacy in your bedroom?

13

10. Whatever happened to Keith Miller's wine?

Finally, if you concede that neither you nor your church can relate to any of this Electric World, then I'm afraid you are average. Feel free to reveal that the person in charge of the Richter scale at your church says he never gets so much as a flick of the dial. I don't mean that all of us are not, to some extent, interested in these superstars. I simply want to assert that they really don't say much that affects us, one way or the other.

With the recent heavy media barrage touting those celebrities who quarterback the blooming born-again phenomenon, I am asking myself one question: *Do they make any real difference in my life or the life of my church?* I keep coming up with a big No. In all my years, I have seen only *one* Billy Graham convert that I could identify as a nonmember of a church before his conversion. He lasted exactly two Sundays as a member of one of our local churches. I have asked many minister friends if they know any converts. The answers have been, "Few, if any."

I know that many converts must be made, because Price Waterhouse-type folks keep telling us so. But the cost per head must be astronomical, compared to the per-capita cost of converts in our garden-variety churches. The old saw "You can't put a price on souls" doesn't seem to fit here. It takes millions to support the life-style of the Electric World. I am saying that the little church in the wildwood must have been doing a pretty good job, because she sure had far less to work with in the way of capital assets. Also, her converts have a higher degree of visibility and continuity.

Most people I know in local churches of any size simply do not understand such things as the conversion of Larry Flynt and his postconversion statements. This fact started to dawn upon me some years ago. I began to discuss candidly with my people what effect, if any, these stars had. I discovered I had some closet Oral Roberts followers who were trying to get over bad experiences brought on by his "have faith" approach. I have witnessed severe crises of faith because of him, especially in terminal cases. I have not seen *one* person who was healed in body through any direct or indirect contact with his work.

I know there are bound to be people who will affirm his approach, but I don't know personally of any church (except Pentecostal) where his ideas have done other than cause strife. Oh, I read about Ruth Stapleton's "healing of the mind" routine. This seems to me to be nothing more than a way to cover up, if the body fails to respond to healing. I simply don't know a soul who has been healed physically in the manner we often hear about.

I once visited a terminally ill young man for three months with at least one lengthy visit each week. I saw him once a day while he was in the hospital. He had been pronounced cured by some zealots with Roberts' literature. When he found out a few days after the "cure" that he was not well, he ran from the hospital in nothing but a gown. In the following weeks he suffered severe depression. I wished that the Roberts people had come to walk with the lad that last mile of the way. But they were nowhere to be found. He simply could not make peace with the "have faith" approach.

Most churches are made up of a cross section of all the basic types of people. They laugh. They hurt. They cry. Sometimes they are lonely in their Christian experience. The world of the smiling media stars in lace cuffs is *not* their world. Oh, I know that occasionally these people will conduct a funeral, such as Humbard did for Elvis Presley, or Graham for Lyndon Johnson. That is still a long way from being in touch with the world of the church on the corner.

I am confident of one thing at this point. Though we read about them, see them on television, and adorn our coffee tables with their latest books, we really can't relate to much these people are saying. The contribution they make is greatly exaggerated by the awesome power of television, radio, and magazines.

I just can't find the masses who are "changed" by Graham, Roberts, Humbard, and others. Those masses never seem to filter down to my church as recognizable persons. Other than enjoying their productions (for those who do), average Christians simply cannot equate their Christian experience with that which is held up before them.

In the December 21, 1977, issue of *Christian Century,* in an article entitled "Denominations: Surviving the '70s," Martin E. Marty has suggested that much of this superstuff is about to peak.

He confesses that he believes strongly in denominational life. He laments that presence of generalized religious blur. His hope for denominations, with all their rich traditions, is that they may prosper again in what he calls new and chastened ways.

Martin is to be thanked for that article, and I pray sincerely that my ideas here will give you a closeup view of life in the churches.

So, if you honestly have felt guilty because you can't translate the Electric World into your life, this book is for you. As is the case with others, maybe you have tried and failed. Cheer up! People are surfacing everywhere who want to go back to something more basic. We have a word for you in your garden-variety congregation and life.

2

Living a Lifetime
Between Cotton Plant
and Forrest City

Tom T. Hall must have known something about Cotton Plant during World War II, when he wrote about "old dogs and children." We had a townful. I never knew about watermelon wine, but there must have been some of it around. The Legion Hut dances were supposed to be off-limits to us kids, at least that's what grown folks thought. Wandering around the Hut on a hot summer night when a dance was in progress, we boys could hear the soothing tones of Glenn Miller. We could also talk to the fellows who came outside to get braced up for the late night chill.

Tom Hall's song describes an old black gentleman giving advice. I can relate to that quite well. Some of the best advice I ever heard was from an old black gentleman. He lived around the corner from us. Our neighborhood was integrated, and we never even knew it. When asked why he was so happy, he replied, "You got to love wherever you are." This made sense even to a twelve-year-old.

That advice has helped me love my churches wherever they have been. From Cotton Plant to Forrest City, I've had a lifetime full of churches, towns, and wonderful people. There is a worldful of folks out there who can identify with me in this. Their lifetimes have been spent between Cotton Plant and Forrest City, or wherever they were and wherever they are.

Why does the world tell us to get away from the small and go to the big? Some people never do, and many seem plenty glad they didn't. Bigness can be a fantasy. When people get to wherever they are going, if they have learned anything along the way, it is this—the only difference between where they were and where they are is simply *more of the same*. That is one of life's greatest lessons.

Oh, I know this is simplifying it too much for some people. But I'm not talking about material things. I'm talking about values, joys, heartaches, stresses, and the challenge of my black friend—to love life wherever one is. It is only human for us to believe that somewhere life is bigger and better. All those big-city churches seem to put the rest of us down just by being there. It's only natural. *We* don't telecast to *them; they* telecast to *us.* If you are always the telecastee and never the telecaster, it is easy to get that second-class feeling.

I'm not knocking the cultural advantages that we miss in our Cotton Plants. However, they are sometimes not as great as they are cracked up to be.

I guess it's only natural to want to get away to what we suppose is better. We had four roads out of Cotton Plant. The ones to Des Arc, Patterson, and Hunter were not paved. The road to Brinkley was paved for four miles to Dark Corner. Gravel carried us the remaining seven miles to Brinkley. The reason the three roads were not paved, even for a stretch, is that they didn't lead anywhere. The only reason folks had for going from Cotton Plant to Hunter was to play ball.

But going to Brinkley was a different matter. Brinkley was on Highway 70, and Highway 70 led to the world! One direction took you to Little Rock, and the other led to Memphis "down in Dixie," as the radio announcer would say. The Peabody Hotel was in Memphis, and everybody's fondest dream was to go to the Peabody, if only to walk through the lobby. Your status was automatically enhanced if you could say you had been to the Peabody.

There was one other place that I always thought I'd like to live, if I had to leave Cotton Plant. That was—you guessed it—Forrest City. Cotton Plant didn't have a swimming pool, and Forrest City did. Although it was only thirty-six miles away, it took over an hour to get there. So we swam in Turkey Creek mostly, and then washed the mud off as best we could. But swimming at Forrest City was a treat of worldly pleasure beyond description.

Though the pool at Forrest City was an occasional orgy of delight, still we all were grateful for Turkey Creek. It was ours, and

it was accessible. When I later asked many of my Forrest City parishioners if they had looked upon their pool the way we had, they were amazed. They had simply taken it for granted. What had been exciting to us had been commonplace to them. Now I realize that the folks at Hunter must have envied us at Cotton Plant. We had Turkey Creek and Smith's Soda Fountain. I jerked sodas for those unfortunate people from Hunter every Saturday.

I don't see a bit of difference in the real world, from one town to the next. The only differences are superficial and cosmetic. Marabel Morgan didn't invent Christian sex. We did that at Cotton Plant at Sunday school parties. We had a game we called "Knock for Love." The girls would get on one side of the door, and the boys on the other side. You would knock the number you wanted, and sure enough, your number would walk out to meet you. Inventive ways were made up to communicate one's number to one's favorite girl, and vice versa. Now and then, someone would get in line ahead of you and rap your girl's number. This was rather traumatic because the rules called for a guaranteed kiss. So it meant you'd end up with potluck!

Love is the same everywhere, and I must say that I still relate better to the Cotton Plant approach than to that stuff Marabel talks about. I don't really know where Marabel finds all those inhibited folks, but there must be quite a number, to judge from her book sales. We took care of inhibitions at Cotton Plant quite early. They did the same thing at Forrest City, or so I am told.

If you can appreciate life wherever you find it, you will learn to love your church, regardless of its size. My family and I have hated to move from each of our towns and churches. But of all the moves in my life, the most painful was when my dad took a job in North Little Rock. Leaving Cotton Plant was hard on a teen-age boy. My mother knew that her three boys had no experience in the big city. After all, a kid could get lost in Chicago, New York, or North Little Rock. We all cried each step of the way. I never forgot that move even later on, when I began to move from church to church. Finally, through many toils and snares and churches, my wife, two daughters, and I arrived in Forrest City.

At Forrest City, we have a McDonald's, and there is a faint

rumor that we will soon have one of those places where it will be necessary for us to wipe one another's chins after each bite. That should about make our material world complete.

It may stun a lot of people on the cutting edge of the theological world to know just how disinterested people in Forrest City are in the so-called top-ten religious issues. All this talk about the Third World is more semantic than real to us. We really don't have to fight off the attacks of the gays; therefore Anita's battle was a big ho-hum. We still think of "Soap" as a bar. We were utterly bored with "Mary Hartman, Mary Hartman." I know the folks who write for television keep trying to depict life for the average person, but they just can't do it. Their attempts have been as silly as the "Carter Country" farce. The reason they can't do it is that they don't understand life as most of us live it. They write about fringes. Then, after so long, the fringes begin to look commonplace. But they aren't. No way.

This is true in the secular field and also for media productions from the galaxy of current religious stars. Normal Christian living isn't much like the images and ideologies presented to us by the Electric stars.

I have a conviction that most of the people we like to call average live somewhere between Cotton Plant and Forrest City. Our lives are never valued for their good qualities. Instead, our churches and ministers are told by inference from the Electric world, via the media, that our lives are dull. We are told that we are not informed, if we are not with the charismatic movement one day or dabbling in experimental worship routines another. We are told that church life in a Forrest City is obviously inferior to church life in a Memphis, because Forrest City is smaller.

Despite these socio-religious games, my own stable church is made up of the same sort of people I have known in all the small towns where I have lived. We don't sit on the floor Indian-fashion and we don't wave our hands around, praising the Lord. We did not even get carried away when the Billy Graham rally hit Memphis. The steering committee for the rally had bombarded every small town within miles with religious "hype." There were all kinds of spinoffs from this. Despite all the furor, only a few followers were picked up here and there. Yet, when they got together in Memphis, the number was large. But that was because they had canvassed hundreds of miles and hundreds of thousands of people. It was carefully planned, and created an illusion of widespread excitement and enthusiasm. Graham's pre-crusade buildup was the key. It is not difficult to understand. His people capitalize on the *power of suggestion*. If enough people are told enough times that it is going to rain, I guarantee you a great percentage will come forth on the given day with raincoats. When a geographical area is saturated with the news that the greatest preacher in the world is coming, and they hear this again and again for months before the advent, a large, well-prepared percentage will come out to greet him. He doesn't have to be Billy Graham. He could be Elmer Dudd from Dewberry Switch, Arkansas (zip pending).

Forrest Cities and Cotton Plants don't have the money or the personnel for this kind of buildup every Sunday.

In the nonElectric church we say the Apostles' Creed, sing the Gloria Patri and Doxology, and we meet at eight forty-five and eleven o'clock for divine worship. We are greatly concerned for the terminally ill in our midst and for a stable environment for our children's religious growth, just to mention two of our never-ending emphases. It is absolutely no different anywhere else, when people pursue basic things. We are all wrestling with the same human dilemmas.

I love it, even though it is not Riverside in New York. It is our church and our town, USA. The problem is that the media have magnified the fringes, both the right and the left. The rest of us are holding court somewhere in between and grateful for it. My arrival is not to a place. It is to a realization that I live with and love what the world calls mediocre. I've learned not to be intimidated by those folks who have a message for us if we will only write in. *We* have a message for *them*. It is about how to be happy and secure without extravagant trappings. They are the minority. *They* ought to be listening to *us*. Who are 'they'? I know. I've met some of them. Some of them have lost their way.

Miss Sue Anna didn't. She moved to Forrest City some years ago, and I preach to her every Sunday.

3

The Day They Ruined "Blessed Assurance"

Now that I have let you know how I feel about local churches, let me tell you when I think we started having trouble. It was when media religion began to gain too much power over our lives.

In 1952, about the only mental picture we had of religious personalities over the airwaves was what I would call churchy. Those were the days before television really got going with the present revved-up Christian personalities. Radio preachers in those days usually came on at night over Mexican stations. Most of those were characters right out of *Elmer Gantry*. There are a few such as John E. Brown and Charles E. Fuller, who made significant contributions. And it must be said that those men broadcast in such a way as to relate to local churches. They were not a threat to the way we went about our work, quite happily including prayer, praise, preaching, and necessary housekeeping. Funds sent to them were turned into schools, and did not support baronial life styles.

On Sunday morning we would hear such churchy-type programs as "The Lutheran Hour," or the fine voice of Ralph Sockman. These complemented our efforts in local churches. The pipe organ music and the singing of familiar hymns were just the needed energy boost that minister and laity alike could feed on. Those programs ministered to us. They hardly entertained us. It was not unusual for Sunday school classes to share the wholesome emphases of these early Sunday morning programs. My, has there ever been a change in Sunday morning coming down! A completely new phenomenon has emerged during the past quarter-century. Unlike Sockman, Fosdick, or even the lesser known radio preachers of old, the present order is now patterning its productions after secular show

24

business, not after the old familiar church service. This change has come about slowly, almost unnoticed. Before it is over (unless feeble efforts like this help to check it), it will transform life in local churches, leaving them frustrated and incapable of functioning in the sensible way that has helped to stabilize American Christianity for two hundred years. I truly believe small churches are in peril at this point. That is, if they model their worship on the star/stage performance level.

My first encounter with this new order was rather innocent, but did it ever signal different trends for local churches! My first appointment was in Plumerville—population 550, according to the city limits sign. Then news that Billy Graham was coming to Little Rock gave us hope that our so-so spiritual journey would get up some steam.

Now friends, Graham was one of our boys who made good. Back in those days, the world at large usually didn't pay much attention to preachers, except those in New York City. But Billy was turning the heads of reporters wherever he went. He was a good old-fashioned Southern Baptist boy, straight from a dairy farm. He had gone to college, but never to a theological seminary. Consequently, he showed little sign of having been thereby corrupted.

On the day of our Sunday afternoon pilgrimage to Little Rock, we were all full of wild anticipation. Besides having me, our church was also blessed by having a layman who knew music. In fact, I always turned over the preliminaries before the sermon event completely to old Lee. Well, Lee and I, and as many others of us as could go, sang "Sweet By and By" all the way to Little Rock. We arrived plenty early in order to be sure we wouldn't miss the choir warmup. One entire section of the stadium was reserved for the choir. And did they ever warm up! There was a fellow named Cliff Barrows, who could command the attention of hundreds of off-key tenors and mountain altos by the magic waving of his arms. I knew Lee was impressed. I could see it in his eyes.

It was quite a sight. Billy came out holding a red Bible and dressed in an aqua sport coat and white buck shoes. He was the grandest looking fellow I ever saw carrying a Bible. He preached,

pacing back and forth like a caged panther, with his long blond hair flowing in the wind. Thousands of people followed him with their eyes, their heads moving back and forth. It must have been a sight for heaven to see. Another rare treat indeed was the way that fellow Barrows doctored-up "Blessed Assurance." That had always been one of my favorite hymns, but he did something for it that certainly insured his immortality in the music world. On the chorus, he had the choir and crowd sing with a pronounced pause after each of the words "This—is—my—story." Old Lee had never thought of that before, but I could see he was catching on quick.

We returned to Plumerville and coasted on the strength of that mountaintop experience for forty days. No one could say that this novice preacher had withstood the impact of Graham on his life. No indeed! I began a steady search for a blue-green sport coat and white buck shoes. It seemed to me that every preacher who had seen Graham was buying red Bibles like mad. They soon had a special supply at the Baptist Book Store. I got one! I still have it, and it brings back many memories of power. Holding up a red Bible with one hand and pointing to the text with the index finger of the other got more attention in Plumerville than I had ever dreamed possible.

But I couldn't outdo Lee. I knew he was going to pull "Blessed Assurance" on us before long. With me dressed as I was, he got the cue. Sure enough, he led the Greater Plumerville Crusade Choir in "Blessed Assurance" with the correct pauses. On the first go-around some of the folks just couldn't catch on and ran right past us. Lee was kind in his rebuke. They just didn't seem to follow his arm movements the way the folks did Barrows'.

That was the beginning, at least for Plumerville, and the end is not in sight. The fact that Graham had more people in his tenor section than made up the entire population of Plumerville didn't phase us at all. We related the bigtime methods to our community as best we could. Back then, we couldn't see that our stability would be threatened. It was an unspoken but common understanding that God wouldn't do the great things for us here that he had done at Little Rock. We revved it up with all we had, but it seemed the effort was as futile as shoveling sand with a hay fork. My attire and Lee's new techniques didn't increase our average attendance of sixty-three souls at First Church, Plumerville.

It may appear to some of you that I am punching sacred cows and being irreverent about God's finest. That is not my intention at all. What Billy and the lesser stars do for God is a thing for which I am grateful. We are probably better off for having them. However, I am greatly perplexed in one area. This solemn fact surfaces after twenty-seven years of observation: *The contribution these people make to the life of the local church and the average Christian is so minute as to be almost nil!* In fact, they actually can be detrimental to local churches of all sizes, and I would like for everyone to realize this. Here are several reasons.

1. They present models of behavior and methods of worship which we cannot assimilate without doing ourselves harm.
2. They make us feel inadequate because the success of their work never seems to peak.
3. They take more than they give. Millions of dollars are funneled into personality cults, and not a cent gets back to the churches from whose members it came.
4. They pitch their performances on such high notes that many of our people conclude that the hometown worship service is dull by comparison, and therefore must be void of God's presence.

This final conclusion is the one which hurts us most. When the local situation is diagnosed as lifeless, many well-intentioned parishioners and ministers seek a resurrection. This erroneous diagnosis leads to attempted cures oftentimes worse than the presumed disease. If we had not had such media influences, we would never have thought we were sick in the first place. Our churches are racked with divisions which have come as a result of these remedies. If we had stayed with the models which fitted us, we would not be in such trauma. Let me say it here, loud and clear—I am not referring just to the evangelical "right." The fringe "left" has also imposed its "cures" on local churches, the result often being utter chaos. We have had enough novel approaches to worship, enough new forms of solemnizing weddings, and enough avant-garde ways to observe Holy Communion to send us all to some funny farm. Now the new Christian Broadcasting Network would have us conduct worship in the form of a Johnny Carson Show. Jim Bakker wants us to sign everything we do with PTL, which means "Praise the Lord." He has probably come up with the cheapest publicity for a "ministry" ever devised by man. Every time we praise the Lord, we are supposed to think of old Jim's show.

Many of these extreme models will only work in large city churches, if indeed they will work anywhere. We have cast off choir robes for blue jeans on the one hand, or long flowing Scarlett O'Hara dresses on the other. Our people have had to sit through far-out verse accompanied by guitars, or All-American Jack and Jenny Armstrong toothy grins. For example, the poor embattled Episcopalians were told by one of their priests at the Charismatic Super Bowl in Kansas City, that within ten years the local Episcopal churches would either be charismatic or extinct! It seems to be fad or finish!

I would bet my tithe on one fact. We would not be writing our own obituaries, had we not been convinced by twenty-five years of media models that we are dying. By trying to follow each fad that comes down the pike, we have committed the worst sin of all. We have just about lost our identity. I have known people in many churches, both pastors and laity, who went dancing off after one thing or another. By and large, they were not the most productive people in those churches. I also know many who always contribute to and attend the traveling crusades, being disenchanted with their local churches. *They have been taught well.*

Grassroots pastors like myself have been muzzled for years. We dared not speak out. We did not want to be accused of speaking against God's greater work. Ironically, almost all the superstars have either insidiously or openly belittled the local pastor. While they steadfastly declare the opposite to be true, the bitter fact is that *they have all gotten well at the expense of our supposed sickness.* The Electric Church is alive and *"well-heeled"* on Planet Earth, and that is really what much of it is all about!

So, let's hear it for the ministers and laity who stay in the ruts and trenches of Christianity. They are changing the world one day at a time. They know what their Lord meant when he compared his kingdom to leaven. When the kingdom works best, it works just that way.

I wish they had left "Blessed Assurance" alone!

4

When the Buses
Run Out of Gas

Back in the sixties, when sex first started to sizzle, and the local churches started to fizzle, a new gimmick for growth arose one morning, with the brightness of the sun. It was hailed by some as the grandest revelation since Moses trudged down Sinai. Of all the panic-stricken trips local churches went on, this was the wildest. It is commonly known as "bussing in the sheaves."

Here again, we are faced with a phenomenon which started with the Electric Church mentality—the old "get your better entertainment here" come-on. I am not sure which great prophet claims to have first suggested this guidance. It could have been a dual or triple revelation, so I will refrain from mentioning names, for fear of denying immortality to someone. The first place I ever heard of it was in Indiana, where some fellow bussed in around ten thousand people for a Sunday school record. This boggles the mind. The average population for towns in Arkansas is probably not a fourth of that. At any rate, one or two other churches began to gain national recognition through the joyful fleets of slogan-covered, used school buses. Since copyrights are not given for gimmicks like this, the field was open to all, and white unto harvest.

A new danger threatened the unsuspecting American public—*being hit by a church bus!* You just don't jaywalk aimlessly anymore in small towns. You might find yourself sacked up on the hood of one of these bigwheelers with your face plastered against "Rolling Along for Jesus," or some such edifying verse. I have witnessed bussing in several towns over the past ten years. It's a serious evangelistic business. You just naturally give church buses a broad path in small towns, because those fellows are intense. Now

this ought to let you know that I am not just a casual observer of the national scene. No, indeed! I am a careful pedestrian on the local stage.

We are now seeing in denominational literature (my own included) booklets on bussing and other services, all designed to show small churches how to make it like the big boys. Unbelievable tricks are designed to attract children. Dollar bills have been hidden on buses. Candy, gum, trinkets, and grab bag surprises are the fare much of the time. Promises of movies, parties, and free lunches are included. Anything to inflate sagging church attendance records. Some of these churches have grown into bonafide Electric churches. This is the ultimate plateau for them.

I have several criticisms of this blossoming carbon-monoxide trend.

First, it is a model of behavior designed by a few large churches in heavily populated areas. It has some degree of justification in an urban area where people are accustomed to being bussed to school, work, and play. It can be a way to save fuel and alleviate congestion in those areas.

This is not the case in smaller towns. To offset the prospect of diminishing returns when the buses are limited to small towns, it is not uncommon to see church buses carrying people from towns thirty miles away. It is a little ludicrous to observe buses from these towns meeting each other on the highway. Each bus is carrying people to worship in the town from which the other bus is coming. This happens *every Sunday*. Somehow, worshiping in the next town is more appealing. This swapping of population is nothing short of weird to those of us who are trying to stay out of the way.

Second, bussing is killing small rural churches. There is nothing Christian about this. Animosity is already beginning to surface between pastors of rural churches and pastors in the county seats. The larger churches have more money to hide under seats, a bigger kitchen for preparing hot dogs and hamburgers, and newer movie projectors. The country churches cannot compete and must endure what is a growing tragedy—the raiding of the countryside on Sunday morning. Already struggling to survive, these rural churches will go the way of rural schools and for the same reasons.

33

Their people don't study or play on the local scene. Now they don't worship there, either. Bussing is a sin of the first order against small, rural churches. *If the money spent to transport these children were given to the small churches to shore up their local facilities, it would say something good about the mission spirit of the larger church.* As it is, the larger church is growing at the same rate the smaller church is dying.

Third, bussing is a violation of the time-honored idea that each local community ought to support its own church. One denomination, in particular, which is now big on bussing, used to declare from the mountaintops that its members should join the congregation closest to them. Bussing has given this advice a hollow sound.

The past saw comity arrangements between pastors. They tried not to proselytize members of another congregation. It was regarded as a sin against the spirit of Christian cooperation to compete for the devotion of people in other parishes. When sticky situations arose, ministers were compelled to inform each other. Bussing is now violating the spirit of that longstanding practice. It is turning church against church and pastor against pastor. Now, when the inevitable differences come between people and their church, they don't seek to work them out. They simply catch the bus to the big church uptown. The small churches have no recourse.

Fourth, I think the main reason bussing caught on was that it enhanced the image of the pastor! It is the most egotistical ploy pastors have used since the invention of bogus doctorates. If this is not true, then why is the pastor's name usually painted on each bus? It reminds me of one of my friends in Little Rock.

Back there in the trolley car days, kids would ride those things for hours with transfers. One fare would do it all. I had a friend whose father owned a prominent business. Trolleys and buses sold advertising space on their sides. This friend's father rented a large spot on the sides of all the trolley cars. The description of the business had his full name followed by that of the firm. My friend was a Jr. It was quite a thrill to sit by an open window with the name of my friend spread all over the side of that trolley car. It was almost like he owned it. We weren't above mentioning Junior's name out loud, so folks would know that a celebrity was on board.

Building bigger buildings and inflating the average attendance by two or three hundred bussed-in children will enhance the pastor's image. The trouble is that a great number of country preachers are donating their blood for the town preacher's transfusion.

Fifth, bussing is irresponsible in this day of limited resources. If we ever have gas rationing, we are going to hear some pretty fanciful arguments to justify this saving of the rural lost sheep. Seldom are the buses filled to capacity. They are notorious for getting poor gas mileage, and the mechanical upkeep and repair costs are astronomical. When the rationing stamps are passed out, the church-bus owners better hope that those handing out the stamps are not members of some of those struggling country churches.

Sixth, and finally, *church life dependent upon bussing is subject to catastrophe if the bussing suddenly stops.* Sanctuary capacity, as well as educational building dimensions, have to be planned for "X" number of people. If these are geared for the inflated numbers brought in by bussing, local churches are headed for trouble in two areas. First, they will find it difficult to pay for all of it. Children do not bring in much revenue, and the kind of parents who send them, being glad for the day-care services, are not about to pay for these services. Second, unless the bussing continues, overbuilt facilities will become a financial burden through lack of use.

Bussing does have one advantage, as I discovered while in the presence of one of the pastors of a nationally known bussing church. A golf match had been arranged, and I was invited to participate. We exchanged comments about our respective churches and discovered we had one thing in common. Both of us had early worship services, as well as one at eleven o'clock. He asked if this were not a tiring experience, to which I gave an honest yes. The fact that I usually face only three dozen people is not the most encouraging way to start the day.

He replied that he knew just how I felt. He only had eight hundred at his early service, and it was almost impossible to be excited by that number. This hardly compared, he said, to the two to three thousand at the eleven o'clock hour. I must admit it. I was awed by his sense of humility, because the last time eight hundred people listened to me was when I gave the invocation at the rodeo. I'm afraid eight hundred people at eight forty-five would swell me like a toad with vainglory and pride. I really hadn't realized bussing had such a humbling effect. He then hit a tee shot about two hundred fifty yards straight down the middle. I promptly sliced one into the local Judean wilderness. All this talent resided in a man several years younger than I. I thought, "Aw shucks, if I had known then what I know now, I wouldn't have sold my aqua coat and white bucks."

5

Being Bullish on Growth
Is a Mistake

The first requirement for both pastors and lay people to be happy in a local church is to find reasons for loving our situation. Closely related to this is our need to discover why we are not, never will be, and should never want to be, Electric. When it dawns on us that the real issues of this life are handled right on our own corner, we will have discovered an abiding love. Happiness, peace of mind, friends who really care and comfort us in the valley of the shadow of death, are the real advantages of local churches. We can't get these things through the mail. The great "on fire" congregations are simply trying to do the same things.

Christ came to solve our human dilemma. There is not a better laboratory for this anywhere than a typical local church. The chemistry there is accessible to anyone. The truthful platitudes may be transmitted by the superstars, but the necessary help comes from our friends on the corner.

The fifties saw local church growth of an unparalled sort. It was mainly through Sunday schools. World War II had scattered us over all the world in body and soul. As a result, we came together in every conceivable kind of group, because we were hungry for one another. Although this was going on in all aspects of life, we in the churches thought it was something we were doing. It was our own creation, we thought. But it *wasn't* a product of the church. It was a product of the *times,* and when the inevitable decline set in, we began to go out of our minds in an attempt to regain what we thought we were losing.

This led to the most insidious trip of all. Our dissatisfaction with the apparent failure of the local church to retain its members

37

resulted in two evils. *First, we failed to analyze the situation properly.* We blamed the wrong things. *Second, we panicked and began a tortuous job of redesigning the church,* according to strange and outlandish models.

Let's think about the first error. Granted that we began to see a loss in some places, that loss was not a factor everywhere. Not every church was losing members. When they did, they did not regress past where they were, before all the foam of the fifties started. The fifties saw balloons, little games people played, slogans of every kind, and a sure and certain belief that the golden age had arrived. We just ran out of slogans and games, that's all! Also, the people who came in during that journey into trivia found other, more tantalizing ways to get their emotional lifts. We had to come forth with something better than that silly string of paper bananas, with the name of each person in attendance. We were "one of the bunch." How could we have been so blind!

We failed to see that the church is strong at its core. I mean by this the real foundation of the church, those people who were there in faithfulness before the surge. These were the ones who stayed through it all. Unwittingly, we measured our "decline" by the loss of the people who gave us our "success." We were wrong on both counts. We should have seen them for what they were, as they came and as they went. We saw multitudes of people join churches, but they really didn't count the cost of discipleship, because we brought them in on a kiddie-show level.

We should have known then what I think we can recognize now. If we can understand the real reasons for the decline, we can see not only where we went wrong, but how we can avoid depression and panic today.

Historically, church decline has come about because of three main factors (obviously, I am leaving out times of international crises such as war and periods of severe persecution against the church).

1. Population decline within the local community
2. Dissatisfaction with pastoral leadership
3. Apathy

Although there could be a combination of all three, it is not usual. In the sixties, we were seeing a legitimate reason for decline, other than the defection of those who came in during the peak days of the fifties. In small towns all over America, there was an exodus of people who were beating a path to the big cities. This had a major effect on the local churches. Instead of seeing this for what it was, we began to increase the tempo of our gimmicks. We hoped to bring back the excitement of the fifties. We should have been ashamed of the cheap methods we used. Ironically, the basic way we had gone about our work and our worship was okay. We simply did not know how to live with population shift.

Population decline *could* account for much of the problem now. Then again, it might not be an outright decline, but a reshuffling of population. Our town is a stable community with about as many people moving out as are moving in. Even with this apparent stability, our church has experienced a *shift* in population resulting in a slight attendance decline.

We had thirteen graduating seniors three years ago, eleven two years ago, and twelve in the last class. This makes thirty-six young people who are still residents of our town and members of our church, but who are away in school or in other preparatory routines. At least twenty-five of their number had been in church every Sunday. Seven of one class sang in the chancel choir. During this period eleven babies were born into our church family.

For every senior who leaves, a baby must be enrolled in the nursery. And these babies will miss church with greater regularity because of sickness or young family mobility. Our congregation has a loss factor at this point that we can measure easily. There is no reason to quote figures, but we ran a study and found that we were doing better than we thought.

Also, we discovered we had another shift which eventually added up to a loss in average attendance. We have people who may still be with us in mind and heart, although they will never be with us bodily again. I refer here to the elderly who were placed in nursing homes or under the care of someone in a private home. We counted this number in with the youth who left us.

Actual deaths had to be taken into consideration. They numbered eleven last year, but we received on confession of faith more than we lost by death, so we were ahead there. Our new members from other churches about equaled our transfers out. All this makes us look pretty typical of thousands of churches in small towns all across America. *It is intended to do just that.* Our study saved us from undue paranoia, excessive guilt, and frustration. We didn't send off for the latest gimmick to shore up a dying congregation. *It was not and is not dying!*

We are bombarded with messages about growth. Everything in our material world tells us we need measurable growth. Yet, while money may make more buildings appear, and build new places to eat, money can't produce babies! Our local church boards meet and unconsciously impose the growth ethic on the church. Some pious soul with the spirit of a medieval crusader will feel that God is not pleased. Then an unfortunate and painful navel-gazing occurs. Eventually a panacea is sought from the media medicinemen.

I'll talk about pastoral leadership later. It *is* a factor of disenchantment. However, it is greatly overemphasized.

The third reason for decline in attendance is apathy. Here is an interesting point. Local apathy *could* be a result of the poor reasoning we have mentioned. For example, if your small-church congregation is going around each Sunday talking about how bad things are, this will just about kill any joy there. People don't want to come to worship and hear Sunday school teachers, ushers, people in the pew, and the pastor talk about how few there are in attendance. These things ought to be evident, unless one is blind.

Apathy can be disgust in disguise. It is important for a nonElectric church to know that it can't ever be Electric. It is important for its members to know that there may be reasons for decline that are out of their control.

I am thinking in particular of one church in a small town. They had an older pastor, at least older than they thought they needed to lead them to the promised land. So they began to analyse their situation. They began to look objectively at the records of the past—the glorious past! And they found that it was not so glorious in many aspects. After that they decided to quit feeling sorry for themselves. But the most important thing they did was to swear off gimmicks. They had tried lay-witness missions, youth-led

41

revivals, a venture into the charismatic jungle, and a Billy Graham film or two. They stopped attendance campaigns and growth emphases. They decided upon a pattern for their church built on a traditional model that was meaningful to them. They chose the stable way of worship and ministry they had experienced years ago. This transformed them overnight. They were happy to quote that psalm, "I was glad when they said unto me, 'Let us all throw away our slogan buttons and bumper stickers!' "

There is a story in the Old Testament about the time that David was chosen to fight the Philistine giant, Goliath. Saul was King of Israel but since he was not about to go up against Goliath himself, he thought that at least he could help the young lad David by suiting him up for battle. Saul chose to dress David in his own armor.

There follow some of the most meaningful words in all literature, especially for the point I am trying to make: "And he tried in vain to go, for he was not used to them. Then David said to Saul, 'I cannot go with these; for I am not used to them' " (I Samuel 17:39 RSV).

Then David went out and slew Goliath with the primitive and basic tool which had brought him that far—a slingshot.

That's the only way local churches will ever kill their Goliaths. The Sauls are always wanting to load their armor on the little Davids. The little Davids are foolish if they buy chunks of it.

6

Since You Can't Have Robert Schuller, Be Content with What's-His-Name

Some years ago, a friend who likes to tell stories swore on his divinity degree that this story is true. It seems that he was in a small-town restaurant somewhere in East Tennessee. A young mother and her son were having difficulty deciding on a choice of food for the boy, a lad in the seven- or eight-year-old bracket.

Each time his mother made a declaration to the waitress for a vegetable meal, he would insist that he wanted a hamburger and french fries. After three or four volleys from each, the experienced waitress said, "Why don't you let the kid have a hamburger and fries?" The mother gave in, of course. (My friend suggested that the waitress knew her kitchen's nutritional potential better than the mother did.)

When the waitress had left, the little kid, flushed with the joy of victory, said as earnestly as he could, "Gee, she thinks I'm real!"

Anyone who has known that particular stage of development in such a child can identify with the poor, defeated mother. In fact, this kind of kid was the only kind my wife and I ever had.

This story embodies the ideas I want to present to you lay people. Your pastors may or may not be kids, but they are *real*. I hope to offer some insight into how you can help them.

If I have heard once, I have heard two million times (another ministerial weakness—counting), "After all, a preacher is only human!" This usually comes after the pastor has been expected to act in a certain way and has failed. I would like to offer some suggestions to every caring layperson. These suggestions can make the difference between merely *saying* your pastors are human and *treating* them that way.

43

·OUR PASTOR·

For you to truly recognize their humanity, you must continually be aware of several things. *First, the pastorate is a very lonely business.* It has an unique loneliness all its own. There is no condition more lonely than to be surrounded by people and not to have any authentic ties with those people. Allow me to illustrate what I am saying.

The small towns and small churches are full of people with extensive family ties. These ties are best observed during festive occasions—Father's Day, Mother's Day, Easter, Christmas, and the Fourth of July. We could add Labor Day weekend and a few others. Here is my point. Most of those days are celebrated in church on Sunday. This is taken for granted by the people in our stable communities, because their parents (or children) are close by for them to visit. When the parents live elsewhere, many of my parishioners leave town to visit them on those weekends. The pastor does not have this option. The last time I spent Mother's Day with my mother was when I was in high school. My wife's last visit home on Mother's Day was the year we married.

Christmas and Thanksgiving are other times when people either go away to their parents' homes or celebrate with them in the local community. All these happy times usually fall on weekends, or so close that the mobility of the pastor's family is nil. Many children in parsonages suffer because they miss the trips other children make to their grandparents. They can't be taken out of school in the middle of the week, and the pastor is on duty on the weekends. Thus, the pastor's family cannot be with those they love most at those special times.

In the cities, there is a mass exodus on those occasions. That is, except for the city pastors. The pastorate is a rootless experience, a fact never more magnified than on those occasions. When I bring this to the attention of laymen in workshops, they are amazed. Most of them determine to do something about it. If you really want to treat your pastor as a human, why not work with your governing board toward granting at least two of these weekends each year for your pastor to leave town?

In one of my churches the board said something to this effect: "We want you to spend at least ten dollars each month in calls to your parents. And we want you to charge it to the church." Some perceptive woman had made a speech before that board years before. She had talked about the estrangement of a pastor on these occasions, and that board had determined to help by strengthening family ties.

Second, your pastor gets tired on the job. He or she is on call twenty-four hours a day. Unlike some doctors, who have answering services and other doctors to relieve them, our small churches have only one minister. There is no associate. As was true in the discussion about festive occasions, mobility is also extremely limited on normal weekends. The idea that pastors are free during the week is a joke. Where will they go? Their children are in school, and if they do go somewhere, unless they visit other members of the clergy, they find people too busy at work to visit with them. Our world works toward Friday. "Thank God it's Friday" doesn't make sense at all to a pastor. This is an occupational hazard of the highest order.

Allow me to point out something you lay people can do to help. Most people are not aware that about the only time parishioners come to a pastor's office is when they have problems. My doctor friends say that four or five days in a row of other people's sicknesses is all they can stand, and then they *have to get away.* I can understand that, and I encourage them to do it.

But pastors can't leave on weekends, so what is to be done? You can make it a habit to take them out for lunch or coffee. Another wonderful thing would be to take both pastor and spouse to lunch. It doesn't have to be more elegant than a fast-food place. The object is to *talk about ordinary things.* It is enjoyable when people come by just to spend some time in my office telling me how well things are going. It is like receiving a gift.

Also, you can *instruct the pastor not to come back for funerals or illness when taking time off.* The weariness of this job is compounded by never being able to make plans for trips. People usually don't choose when they have heart attacks. I have canceled football games, vacations, and one-day trips so many times that uneasiness, like a cloud, hangs over every planned trip. Some other pastor can fill in for your pastor. After all, your favorite doctor is not always

46

accessible, and you allow his associate or his substitute to handle
your emergency. Then, when something happens in *your* family,
be big enough to use the substitute pastor yourself. This will set the
example for others.

Third, grant pastors the right to be sick on Sunday morning. Be aware
that they are in a show-must-go-on business. Pastors have
conducted services under the most excruciating conditions. Other
occupations have a way out. There is no way out when it is nearing
eleven o'clock, and your head is splitting because of a sinus
infection. If you take medicine for pain, you can't think because of
the *medicine,* and if you don't, you can't think because of the *pain.*

When your pastors are not alert, it could be nothing more than a
headache. Be sparing in your criticism of their poor efforts. Pastors
don't usually like to announce during the call to worship that they
are about to throw up. This kind of announcement is hard on the
organist's artistic sensitivity. The congregation can pass the word
when they know this is the case. They can say, as some have said to
me, "Don't worry about it. Cut it short, and leave it up to us to pass
the word. We understand."

Fourth, pastors have constant pressure from the need to be living examples
of all they say. When they give advice (and much of preaching is
advice), they are under pressure to live up to the letter, not just the
spirit of it, or they are subject to criticism. This is a very heavy
weight. One way to help them break out of this god-role is simple.
Here it is. *Call them by their first names!* This is not disrespectful.

Sometimes, without realizing it, pastors take themselves too
seriously. This tendency can be greatly relieved by a show of
personal love, in the simple act of calling them by name. When I go
to a new pastorate, it is a warm experience when one of my people
says something as simple as, "Merle, I want to know you better.
I'm coming by to see you." This has always helped me to turn down
the glow of my halo.

Fifth, pay attention to their children. They probably don't have
uncles, aunts, and grandparents nearby, so be one to them. Pastors'
kids are sometimes "bad" because they are *lonely* or *left out.* Always
remember that a rootless, lonely life breeds frustration.

Sixth, the pastor doesn't have a minister. You do. There were times when I would have given anything to have a pastor to talk with. I'm sure my wife has felt somewhat the same. I am not speaking of problems. I am thinking of just being able to hear someone else's ideas. No one gets more tired of the same old preacher than that same old preacher and his family. This may come as a shock to some of my people, who tell me I am the world's greatest preacher. I know I'm not! I am sorry to disappoint them, but I would hate to have to listen to my ideas each week. Come to think of it, I do, and it's terrible!

Every local church can solve the problems I have mentioned. All that is needed are some insightful, caring, lay people. Your pastor may very well respond by saying, "I can't believe it! You people think I am real!" Quit saying they are only human, if you don't mean it.

7

Take Your Bulletin
to That Big Church Preacher
Every Time You Bring His Home
to Your Preacher

I suppose it is about time for me to justify all this talk about average churches and average pastors. One of the aspects of writing that distresses me is that most book critics live in and around electrifying situations. They live in the cities. They attend (if they do attend) Dr. Ivemadit's church in downtown Maxiapolis, where the heads of corporations kneel side by side in endless rows. Their church is not necessarily an Electric church—however, it might have aspirations to be.

These critics would never go to a church where the two biggest communicant tycoons own maximum-capacity chicken houses. It was refreshing for the world to look in on Plains, Georgia. The thing that stunned the big-city reporters was not that a President worshiped there. The thing that kept coming through the reporters' words on the five o'clock news was the simple fact that the church *was there at all!* Those fellows were stunned by that way of life. They were puzzled that this kind of church hadn't applied for a place on the visitors' tour of historic sites long ago.

Now, for some more facts. United Methodism is the second largest Protestant denomination in the world. Get ready for this, you top-ten-issue lovers—almost seven out of ten of those churches have fewer than one hundred people at the Sunday morning worship service. Southern Baptists are the largest single denomination. Though a majority of their churches average over one hundred in attendance each Sunday, still the chief issues that confront them are tied to the local scene.

As for the Presbyterians, Episcopalians, and others, the percentage of churches averaging over one hundred is probably

even smaller. A great many pastors of all denominations are overjoyed to report that they have preached to one hundred people, even on Easter.

I always camp around the book displays at the conference, like a fisherman in a still pond. (Now and then I'm asked to autograph one of my "best sellers.") One sharp young pastor turned to me last year and said, "Merle, I can't use any of this stuff on church growth. This display is depressing." He wanted so badly to be a successful pastor in Wagon Springs. But there wasn't a thing on that table that could help him where he lived and worked. He wanted just a few ideas—not many—simply a few workable suggestions for himself and his people. Instead, all he found were books on how to enjoy life in the Electric whirl.

With this in mind, you lay people should understand that there is not much help for your pastors in the very places they need it the most. You can do as much for them as any one of the "authorities." Let me tell you about the bulletin game. I'm sure that city critics who write on religion will think I have dropped a marble out of my sack. I expect this to be a revelation to them.

My first three churches couldn't afford that exhilarating luxury called a church bulletin. This is a simply constructed creation which allows those in the pew to know ahead of time what hymns you are going to sing. Sometimes it becomes a check-off device for the kids, telling them how much more misery is to come. I would always have a few families each year who, upon returning from trips to the outside world, would bring me bulletins from churches they had visited. For some of them, this was more than merely to let me know they had been to church. It was a kind of "let us show you how the big boys are doing it" maneuver.

Early in my ministry I had an all-consuming ambition to be pastor of a church with a printed church bulletin. Somehow, that was a symbol I could savor like good food. Of course, I wasn't asking God for offset stuff. I dreamed only of a mimeographed bulletin and being able to pay some high school kid to run it off. My first secretary was just that—a high school kid who worked for two hours Saturday afternoon on the church bulletin. I can't tell you the sense of sheer power that came over me when that girl would stick her head in and ask such crucial question as, "Shall I say that you are to attend the pastor's aid society meeting?" I would give her a yes or no and then dismiss her with, "That's all, Miss Quattlebaum." People coming and going at one's beck and call was enough like wine to cause severe drunkenness at that stage of my life.

I soon graduated to bigger churches, but I found that some of the laity play a game calculated to sober up the most power-drunk preacher. It is called "the big church bulletin against the little church bulletin." (Now, I know that all my people who ever brought me a bulletin will head for the aspirin bottle and determine not to send me a Christmas card next year.) Somehow it seems impossible for pastors to get away from the bulletin game unless they are "at the top." There, they never get bulletins. Their biggest problem is to print enough for visitors to take back home to their own churches. One of my greatest dreams was that one day someone would take my bulletin to an even smaller church to show that preacher how we successful preachers did it.

I can better illustrate this with a true story. Once I was brought a bulletin by a man who said these words: "Now and then, my wife and I just have to get away on the weekends. We always go over to the city, take in a movie, and eat out at a good restaurant. But the highlight of the trip is to go to First Church and hear the emminent Dr. Manywords preach. I could listen to him all day. I brought you one of his bulletins."

My first impulse was to make an airplane of the bulletin and fly it like a bird of paradise up his pulsating nose. I've heard this same put-down more times than one can imagine. Because of this, I say to my friends from Round Pond, "Don't ever tell your minister you just have to get into Forrest City to hear me once in a while. And for God's sake don't take home one of my bulletins."

There is a terrible irony in all this. I admit that preachers' abilities differ. But it is not another preacher's ability that some layfolks are looking for. They are trying to impress people with *their mobility*—that they are able to flee to Plainville, USA, and touch the better world "out there." They wouldn't think of telling their local cafe owner they just had to get away from the food. They don't say to their local merchant that they just have to get away to finer merchandise. And yet, some people will pay more for the same merchandise in Memphis that they could get in Forrest City, in addition to the cost of the gasoline for the trip. Somehow, the label is worth it. The label on the coat from Memphis is like the bulletin from the big Memphis church.

Where does this put your pastor? The only recourse is to think, "If I am ever to be respected by *these* people, I've got to get out of here as quickly as possible." I hate to have some children of local parents come back home for a visit. They have that certain air that suggests: "I belong to the big church in the city. We do it this way. Our *fourth* assistant down the line handles thus and so." Mamma and Dad stand by and smile because they are sure I'm taking notes.

Remember this fact. In most small churches there are only two kinds of pastors. One is the young pastor who will not be with you long. The other is the older pastor, who may be as high up the ladder as he will go. When you bring home "news from the Electric world," you will force one of two reactions:

1. The young pastor may become more ambitious than ever, as well as more restless. If you love him and want him to stay, I assure you, you are packing his bags!
2. An older, less mobile pastor will feel rejected, depressed, and inferior. He can't make it to the big church. He never will, and *he knows that*. Now he also knows that you "have to get away from him for a breath of fresh air," and his heart is mercilessly torn apart.

Please allow me to offer three suggestions to you lay people who care.

First, cease doing things that tend to place your pastor in a bad light. You may never have a "great" pastor in your small town. You *can* have a gracious and godly one, if you help him assess his real worth.

Second, stop confusing big with beautiful. As a black preacher friend said, "Black may be beautiful but it ain't colorful." That was great wisdom. Black had its limitations, and he wanted his people to know it, in order that they might not rest on slogans, *but get busy and work for their race.*

One Sunday a parishioner, who was a frequent "get away" visitor to the big churches and big events where Christians gather, stayed around after the service to speak to me. He looked at me in a rather puzzled way while others were shaking my hand. I knew that my zipper was not the culprit, because I had on a robe. I couldn't understand his stare.

When we were alone he said, with the shocked look of a person who has just seen his first X-rated movie, "Sally and I were in Bigtown church last Sunday, and Dr. Knowsit quoted your book. Sally and I were astounded. Say, where can we buy a copy?"

The point I am making is not that I have been fortunate enough to write. So have many other small-town pastors. My point is—a big-time preacher quoted *me!* Not the other way around. The value system of that couple was in shock!

Third, find some good quality about your church that you missed while you were visiting the Electric church. Don't bring your pastor a bulletin unless you want to show him how those folks could learn from your church at home. There are few things more boring than a church bulletin. It's about as interesting to your pastor as touring the rest room facilities of another church's elementary department.

Let me tell you about a guy I love. He and his wife went to one of the big-name churches. When they came home he said, "Hey, Merle, I listened to that clown for thirty minutes, and he rambled all over the world. I don't know, in the name of good sense, how he ever got where he is—must be a good politician! We really missed you." I know he stretched the truth, but he wanted to make a point.

I worked harder the next week than I had worked in years.

8

Treat Your Pastor
the Way You Treat Your Doctor,
If You Care As Much for Him

After all these years in the pastoral ministry, one thing is as sure as the old adage about death and taxes. I have given up my dream that people will call their pastors when they need them. Somewhere back in the primeval past, the notion was generated that pastors have extrasensory perception, that they can read minds. This is simply not so. Every one of my churches has had members who made me guess when they needed me.

In my present church, it got so bad that I brought it to the attention of my board. They passed a resolution stating that, unless people asked for me, I was not to feel guilt or experience censure if I didn't call on them. Of course, most of the time I find out about illness or bereavement. However, there are occasions when everyone thinks I know, and no one tells me. Many of these occasions result in people having their feelings hurt. This problem causes more stress than you lay people can imagine, but your church can *completely eradicate* this stress, and I guarantee that it will be looked upon as one of the most productive accomplishments in pastor-parish relationships ever undertaken. Simply suggest that your board, vestry, or session pass a resolution, and have a carefully worded announcement extensively circulated, with the information that *the pastor must be informed when he or she is needed.*

Second, ask your pastors specifically to come (or go to the hospital as the case may be) *and tell them exactly what you would like for them to do.* One day I had a call from one of the members of my church. She said, "Merle, Mother is in the hospital in Little Rock. We are not telling many people, and we knew you might not find out. I wish

you would go and talk with her about her attitude toward life. She is hostile because she thinks she has had bad luck."

I had just put the phone down when the secretary said, "Did you know about Mrs. ———? In our women's meeting last night it was whispered to me that she and her family were really hurt because she had been in the hospital for a week, and you did not call on her." It so happened that much of that week I had been in the bed with the flu and had been out of circulation.

No one in the second woman's family had called me. They had not even known that I was sick myself, and I really doubt if they cared. It made my job so much easier when I could go to Little Rock and address myself directly to a woman whose needs had been spelled out for me, knowing that I could be of help. I felt nothing but frustration with the second situation.

Also, there are those wonderful people who will call and say, as one did last year, "My wife is going in for an appendectomy. We will be in Memphis three or four days, and we better not see your head in her room. You have more to do than run over here to say hello. If something critical comes up, we'll call you." He then added, "You better have something to say next Sunday morning. I'd rather have you prepared to say something to me next Sunday than loafing around there in the hospital." Those are the people who make it all worthwhile.

My advice for you lay people is to call your pastors yourself. Don't wait until the word filters down to them. It just might not get there. If you don't call, then don't get your feelings hurt when they don't come. You never become angry when your doctor fails to read your mind. Why should you expect it of your pastor?

In the third place, thank your pastors as you would thank others. Once I sat up all night in a hospital after driving thirty miles in a snowstorm. Indiana snows can be bad. The patient died at six o'clock in the morning, but the family didn't know it. I did. The nurse told me privately. The doctor didn't come until seven o'clock. The family oohed and aahed about the ten minutes the doctor spent with them "so early in the morning." The nurse and I just looked at each other. I am not putting doctors down. I don't know how they keep from going nuts! That doctor had gotten to bed late, and he couldn't have helped the man when the nurse called. He needed the extra hour of rest.

My point is that I was treated as if I were obligated to be there—as if it was something I owed that family because they had paid their "dues," and it was time to collect. Many pastors have been barely thanked for endless hours and trips to hospitals. Thank your pastors with personal letters. You can't begin to realize what a simple note will do for their sense of worth. It will help them, and it will help the total complexion of your pastor-parish relationships.

Last, complain to your pastors the same way you complain to your doctors. That's right, I said complain! Don't complain behind their backs. If they are not getting around to whatever it is you need, tell them. I can illustrate this. When a person is ill, pastors never know when to pray at the bedside. The patient, under the influence of drugs, could mistake prayer for the last rites, and panic. I have seen this happen.

Also, we never know when to talk with people about dying. Once I had a man call me and say, "Pastor, my mother loves your visits at the hospital, but she says you never offer a prayer. She sure would like for you to do that." I explained my position of having to feel around in the dark, and he said he certainly understood. I prayed with her each time after that, until she died. This simple and honest phone call helped me do my work.

My closest friends have been in the medical profession. I have seen them labor under unbelievable circumstances. They were taken advantage of for so long that they learned to be detached. They deserve our respect and consideration. It is no wonder that they understand the problems of the ministry better than any other group.

Treat your pastors the way you treat your doctors. You will be surprised how proficient they will become in their pastoral duties toward you and your loved ones.

9

Don't Make Such a Big Deal Out of Which Punch Bowl He Should Go To

Have you ever been where the preacher's-punch-bowl game is played? The barrier of inviting the pastor to Christmas parties finally having been broken, we now find another dilemma. The host is going to have spiked punch, so what does this sin-convicted soul do? Will he allow his virtuous pastor to stumble into the long line before the questionable bowl? There is a good chance that will happen, because that is where the crowd is. Now the game begins. To save the pastor from corruption, the host announces heartily in the hearing of everyone, "Hey, preacher, your bowl is over here!" Then he points to a part of the room where the only human is some sweet old soul with a grin on her face. There she stands, ready to pour a cup of the most terribly sweet concoction any human ever made. It is obvious little time was spent mixing that stuff. It also becomes obvious that her part of the room is as isolated as a viral ward!

The last time that happened to me, I said, "Save it for your mother-in-law. You made more promises to her than to me. If she thinks you can handle the other bowl, maybe I can, too!" The poor guy had told me how his mother-in-law hated alcohol, and that he hid it when she came. He will never talk that loudly to a preacher again.

I have been led to syrupy sweet punch bowls all my life. It has always been done with great fanfare. I had to make my way through a crowd of my own parishioners who, like Lot of old, "lingered." While Lot lingered outside the city of Sodom, these characters had lingered by that other punch bowl. However, even worse is to be invited to one of those parties that have staggered times for certain

people. We can be sure the subject matter will be as sweet as the punch. My wife and I are to come between the hours of such-and-such. A Gideon will amble up and discuss how many Bibles he has placed in motel rooms. Or some well-meaning person will bend my ear about having just completed a Garner Ted Armstrong Bible Course of six installments. The time of my life is had at these events. As I leave, I can't help noticing that the complexion of the party is going to change in a hurry, because I recognize some of the back-pew crew arriving.

I have three suggestions. *First, help your ministers fulfill themselves as social beings.* Don't isolate them and their punch bowls. Allow them to choose their own way of life. Invite them to your parties. If you think you would be uncomfortable with them and their husbands or wives, you just might be wrong, or your party could be off base for a Christian.

I mentioned the festive times of the year earlier—those times when the pastor's family has to stay in town. You probably don't realize how isolated the parsonage couple feels when they are never invited to parties at such times as Christmas. This is especially true for young people who are in their first pastorates. Small towns all have groups which socialize together, and that is fine. Yet the young parsonage family has no such group. I am at the age when I would rather go to bed early (a sure sign I'm over the hill), but in our earlier years we, like many young couples, felt left out.

My second suggestion is to treat pastors as self-employed professionals. This is the way the Internal Revenue Service looks upon them. Pastors pay their own self-employment tax. My point is this. Every church has leaders. These leaders are usually the town and community fathers. They are powerful people locally and *they know it.*

The hazard of this is that the young (or old) ministers may be looked upon as hired hands. They are only the straw bosses. The real bosses are the fellows who are powerful in the community. The best way I know to lose those fine young pastors you love is to treat them like your well-meaning but inexperienced children. There may be a time for that but it should *not* be done publicly. You wouldn't think of treating a young doctor that way. In fact, small towns will usually build a young doctor an office and guarantee him a high income.

Remember, your pastors may have the equivalent in professional training as doctors! When you disagree with them, show them the respect that is due their education and their profession. In this way you can help them look upon themselves as self-respecting beings of worth.

Last, find some excelling virtue in each of your ministers, and keep it before you when the liabilities loom large. You can't have pastors who are great in every respect, because your *churches* are not great in every respect. If you have such diamonds, they won't be with you long. I don't know of any pastor who doesn't have some excelling virtue which can bless a local church and community. I once knew a minister who couldn't preach interesting sermons. He tried, oh how he tried. But his people loved him anyway. One day one of his caring, thoughtful congregation put a stop to some virulent criticism of him with these words: "Joe may not preach like Ronald, but Ronald never did know my youngest daughter's name. Joe knows the name of every dog in our church!"

It is no wonder preachers seek fake doctorates and every other vestige of prestige they can find. Sometimes a satisfying identity is hard to come by in the pastorate. One is not a person, but "the preacher." Gimmicks are sold constantly to people who are seeking self-worth. We got it from the medical people. I used to wonder why doctors had all those waiting rooms. Now I know. It is so they can have some place to hang all those diplomas for two-week trips to the Rockies, where they took advanced courses on how to dress planter's warts!

The "Who's Who" organizations are the latest gimmick. While writing these words I received a notice to the effect that I had been nominated for inclusion in a *Who's Who* of international fame. The clowns who got up that thing said I was one of only 140,000! They must be out of their minds. I wouldn't join anything for which I have to pay my hard-earned money, just to share my fame with 139,999 other souls! I joined one such "select" group fifteen years ago. Then I paid my advance cut-rate price of $29.95 for an "insider's" edition. They had my name, the fact that I was born in

Damascus, Arkansas (which is right), my parents' names, my wife's name, what I did for a living, and the revelation that I usually voted Republican. I had been led to believe that I was joining a select group of world-changers! The book described hundreds of other similar greats. The only problem was that I needed a magnifying glass to read it.

Help your pastor be a person. Let him pick his own punch bowl!

10

If You Think
a Refund Is in Order,
Say So

There is one thing about churches that I never realized in my youth. Somehow, I thought that people *had* to go, and *had* to support them. I thought the church was like the government. This misunderstanding carried over well into my pastoral career. Some pastors never completely liberate themselves from this misconception. It was helpful to me finally to grasp that only the people's love for God makes them put up with the stuff we preachers impose upon them. I began to appreciate my people more when I eventually became aware that they do not have to be in church; they could be out camping or fishing. They are not forced under pain of a death decree to listen to my golden tones on Sunday. They could tune in one of the stars on a portable television, as they sit by the lake.

You people have invested thousands of dollars over the years in your churches. It is staggering to realize just how much you contribute. *You have the right to your input.* Exercise that right! I want to list four areas in which you can help your church and pastor.

The first concerns the sermon from the lay point of view. Are you being shortchanged in the sermon? We preachers have a Mount Carmel-type pride. Sometimes we feel like Elijah—we can give orders to slay all the foes of God. Not too many folks argued with Elijah the day he brought down fire. We feel the same way, all too often.

Pulpit Digest once had a cute story in a section called "The Ahem Corner": A young preacher looked up from his reading and

64

said to his wife, "How many great preachers do you think there are?"

She answered, "I don't know, but there's one less than you think!"

It is difficult for us pastors to be critical of ourselves, especially of our sermons. This is true for a number of reasons, at least one of which is legitimate. The laity probably doesn't realize how often Sundays roll around. When preachers are constantly pushed by thoughts of the next Sunday's pulpit fare, they sometimes don't have time to assess adequately the faults of the one for the past Sunday. It is easier to polish and correct speeches which are delivered once a month. This is especially so if it is the same speech. Having to create a new sermon each week is something no one can appreciate unless he has to write a new speech every week *for the same people!*

Having said that bit in defense of my troops, let me put lay people back on the offensive. *If your pastors are not producing—tell them.* We preachers go through many, many changes in our thinking. I have a banker friend in his seventies who is something of a cracker-barrel philosopher. He is a good one. He says that the human mind changes distinctly about every ten years. I believe he is right, but I'm certain preachers change more often than that. (I'm in the middle of one right now, and the transition period is so enjoyable I think I'll *stay* in-between.)

One of my changes came right after I received my union card from seminary. I was determined to enlighten my people regarding the last detail of each technical biblical point I broached. I began a series on the Sermon on the Mount. After studying that section of the Bible with all the powers of my superior skills, I was dead certain that our Lord must not have intended to be so simply understood. I concluded that there must have been a mass of hidden meanings in the sayings. I began to quote every authority who ever wrote the word "beatitude." I got more salt out of the "salt" passage than Morton produces in a year. I was certain that my people would be able to camp on whatever theological ground they chose, because I gave them a multitude of alternative campsites.

This spirit-endowed approach lasted for about five weeks. I did notice that my wife was hiding in the Sunday papers immediately

after lunch, but I considered that was probably just her way of relaxing after a morning of heavy thinking.

One Monday, a wonderful man asked me to have coffee with him. He was a genuine friend who had shown his love many times. Eventually we got around to Sunday's service. He clumsily began to tell me that it was difficult for him to be very interested in the alternative views of a couple of German authorities. Of course, I attributed this to the fact that he had not had informed ministers before, and that, like some medicine, it might not be too pleasant, but it was good for him to know these things. Anyway, I was anxious to prepare my people, should they need these ideas when they went to McGehee (the cultural center of our section) for Bible studies. When my friend saw that I was still under the hypnotic influence of my own wonderful grasp of the subject, he said, "Merle, let me put it this way. You are boring us to death!" Now friends, if you don't think that will chill hot coffee, you are crazy!

He thanked me for working so hard, and said the people loved and appreciated me. He said further that all that technical stuff wouldn't help old Homer pump gas a bit. Homer, our head usher, had a thriving gas station. It seems that he had been the first to fall asleep. To this day, I never prepare a sermon without asking myself, "Will these details help Homer pump gas on Monday morning?"

If your pastor is off on a tangent, go to him. First set his mind at ease. Then tell him person-to-person what you really feel.

Second, if you think your church is short-changed in its pastoral leadership, say so. There could be some way you can help. There are times when your pastor may have motor problems. All the rest of the world does, why can't he? There may be times when he just doesn't seem to function well, is not as alert, and does not show the proper interest. The real reason could be depression over legitimate troubles, or almost any problem anyone else might have.

Perhaps there is marital trouble. There could be trials with his children. There might be financial stress. Remember, a pastor is one of the human race, subject to the same toils and snares as anyone else. These kinds of problems can carry over into one's work. It's the same for a minister. The difference is the high visibility of the job. The ministry is like a fish bowl, and it becomes agonizingly apparent when the pastor is floating on the top, with gills flared and barely moving. Don't draw hasty conclusions. It may *not* be time for him to move on.

When my youngest brother was killed in an automobile wreck, I felt something I had never experienced before. Unless people go through these things themselves, they can be only casual observers from a distant mountain. When they do endure such times, they actually feel the chill of the canyon floor. For several months, I could not function. Fortunately, I had a few friends I could talk with. They became my pastoral advisors.

My wife and I were surprised when the people at Siloam Springs sent us on a vacation the next Christmas. One of the congregation told me later that it was specific therapy. The fact that he was a doctor was not as important as his studied efforts toward a better understanding of my mental anguish. This man is a careful student of the human dilemma. They didn't tell me they had noticed I was depressed. They didn't tell me I wasn't functioning. If they had, I would not have taken the trip. They knew that. I would have tried to work harder and would have gotten in deeper. You can take a lesson from these wonderful people. Your pastors bleed just like you do. What makes you think they could get over some tragic death any better than you could? If you are being shortchanged on leadership, it may be because your pastor has some private problem. It may be unknown, but it can be just as debilitating in its effect.

Third, if your pastor is off on a tangent crusading for a "cause," throw out a lifejacket. The poor dummy might drown. We preachers are notorious crusaders. We are compulsive "worthy cause" addicts. I think the real reason is the sense of power it gives us, but I'll leave that to the psychiatrists.

During my seminary days I knew a pastor who would turn off his television set every time a beer commercial came on. Then he would time the thing, and switch the set back on. The poor dunce never knew why he replaced more picture tubes than all the rest of the folks in Dustbowl County put together. He started a campaign from the pulpit for his people to join him in this pursuit of the Holy Grail.

A member of his board kindly told him his convictions were deeply appreciated, but that he was doing much greater damage to his overall work than he could imagine. To the pastor's credit, he took the helpful advice. If that caring layman had left the poor fellow alone to simmer in coffee-break jokes all over town, irreparable harm would have come to the church and to the man.

In the last place, *if you are short-changed in every respect, ask your pastor to leave.* You didn't read that wrong! The pastoral ministry is like any other job. There are some real losers in my profession. They are lazy, they are dishonest, and they couldn't be jogged out of their ruts with a cattle prod. They should shape up or be shipped out. If you have done all the things I have mentioned and more; if you have prayed and languished long, and nothing has happened; then it is time to use the machinery for removal honestly and sincerely, and get on with it.

Each denomination has its backdoor policy. It should. We pastors have no right to sit on the top of Sinai out of reach, just because we wear one of Aaron's robes. Ask for your money back if you are completely short-changed. You deserve it.

So there it is, you may not have Robert Schuller or Norman Vincent Peale, but you may have a very fine man or woman who can be better than you ever thought possible—with your help.

11

You Asked for It, You Got It, Now Drive It

I think it's important to speak to everyone, when revealing some of the inside dynamics of my colleagues and myself. Therefore, even though I am about to address shoptalk in the next few chapters to my brother and sister ministers, I want to include you lay people —after all, you are all Christian ministers in the broad sense. Therefore, here are some suggestions for the pastor in charge. My credentials are in order, because I am one of you. My experience has been limited to balky mimeograph machines, county fairs, and three-traffic-light towns. Comparing the number of traffic lights is a game United Methodist preachers play after every change to a new church. I know that the 70 percent bracket includes all of us traffic-light counters for whom I am writing these chapters.

You can be happier where you are, and that is why I offer these words.

Sometime back there, God spoke to our hearts in some manner. Regardless of how it came about, you and I committed ourselves to the Christian ministry. We *all* went into it blind. I have never yet met any ministers who said they had anticipated what they now experience in the pastorate. This business is simply not what it appears to be.

When we go through all those years of preparation and finally arrive at our destination, we all feel as if the porter must have put us off at the wrong station. Bishop Gerald Kennedy was fond of telling about Rhode Island's late Senator Green. Once a hostess at a dinner party caught him looking at his datebook. She asked, "Senator, are you looking to see where you are going next?"

The old man looked up and said, "No, I am trying to find out where I am now."

When it becomes apparent that the "little English curate" image is a lot of baloney, it is a rude awakening. It is a far cry from a seminary in a big city to Toad Suck Ferry Church.

The shock is further compounded by attitudes we never knew existed. I remember an incident in my student church in Indiana, when my wife and I were having coffee with a family, after services one night. The discussion eventually got around to the future career of the twelfth-grade son of the home. Doing what I thought St. Paul would do, I suggested that he might pray about studying for the ministry. Without so much as a rattle of the coffee cup, the mother replied, "Oh, no. He is much too intelligent for that!" My wife and I were dead certain that the porter had put us off at the wrong station!

That is about as bad as the remark of a woman who shook hands with Henry Sloane Coffin, following the service one Sunday. "Dr. Coffin, you do not know what a help your sermons have been to my husband since he lost his mind!"

Somehow, that is just not where we thought the ministry *was at*. So what do we do? We complain. We are probably the number-one complaining profession in all the civilized world. Complaining is a contagious disease. Its worst result is that we take ourselves too seriously and believe these complaints. We then become impotent in our work. Brother or sister, whatever this business is, you asked for it, you got it, now drive it. You are hardly prepared to do much else.

But another ailment is our number-one malady. That is *paranoia*. Paranoia is the deadly suspicion that someone is after you. The ministry suffers greatly from paranoia. Sometimes there are situations which are legitimately responsible for this feeling. I will admit that. However, in a great many cases we overdo it.

I want to mention one frustration you can rid yourself of to lessen that paranoia. Some of your people want their former pastors, or other local pastors, to preach funerals, and marry their sons and daughters. We pastors get in more of a stew over these occasions than over any other aspect of our ministry. We can't expect to be

thought of in one year by that twenty-year-old engaged girl in the same way she thinks of her former pastor. Why should we expect to? Yet we do, because our egos are at stake.

I discovered a long time ago the freedom that comes by *insisting* that former pastors come back, if the situation tends in that direction. Those people who want them back may be (and most of the time are) innocent of malice. They do *not* intend it as a slap in their present pastor's face.

In almost every town where I have lived, there is a preacher who has grown up in that community. Usually, he will have another means of support. I have such a friend now. His name is Floyd Cowan. He is a Baptist preacher who also is the county tax assessor. I think the world of that man. He knows every tree stump in our county. Floyd has more funerals of all denominations than the rest of us put together. Sometimes we are called on to assist him. Most of the time we are not.

I look on Floyd as a valuable asset. He gets to the hospital ahead of me many times. Politicians have their ways of finding out things. That man is the soul of honor. He would never do anything unethical, and we all know it. You may know such people. They may be retired preachers. Why don't you swallow your pride and allow them to help you in your work? They can become your best friends. Allowing them to help you will also help you defeat your worst malady—paranoia.

If paranoia is our worst malady, laziness is our greatest temptation. Because our schedules aren't exact, we tend to become the most undisciplined souls in the ranks of educated people. Laziness is our besetting sin! I have two suggestions on this point—they are simple, but they work.

First, unless it is your day off, *put on a tie* (or the female equivalent), *shine your shoes and dress up.* A certain standard of dress is expected of those in our position. If you don't wear a tie, for goodness sake, don't look as if you are getting ready to go to the tennis courts. If you look that way, chances are that is where you will routinely end up. There is a self-discipline reflected in dress. It spills over into everything you do.

Second, stop calling your office a study. That communicates to your people a place to prepare sermons. Many of them already think that is all you have to do. *Call your place of work an office.* Publish the office hours where people see them. I guarantee you, they will soon quit running someone's legs off answering the phone at home. Soon they will realize that you do more in that room than dream up your three points and sad story for Sunday.

12

Quit Saying You Are Going to Stay and Praying that You Can Leave

One of my Baptist pastor friends tells me it is a sure sign an old boy is feeling "led to go" to that other church, when he starts printing accolades to his people in the bulletin. This is to insure that the tragedy of his leaving will be more pronounced and that the going-away love gift will be greater.

It makes no difference which denomination we have in mind, the issue is the same. One unfortunate characteristic of local pastors is that, all too often, they are never really happy where they are. It is a disease particularly virulent among United Methodism. Many of our lads and lassies never unpack!

Heretofore in this book, I am certain I have led some people astray. Many of you may have felt that I am envious of the large church and am merely articulating this bitterness. *You have missed the point completely.* I am not attacking large churches or highly successful pastors. I am simply making an effort to warn smaller church pastors and their laity against taking these situations as models for their own growth. If we allow ourselves to be influenced by them, our small churches will become unstable and insecure. Our pastors will grow despondent and depressed. I would like this book to be of help in that area.

If we in the small and average-size churches will accommodate ourselves to our limitations, we can become more productive. One major by-product would be the quieting of ministerial desires always to be moving to greener pastures. One of the causes of this kind of stress is our tendency to focus on methods which don't really help us, coming from the large churches or from the media Electric church models.

While preparing these pages, I was shocked to see that my timing is getting better. In *Time,* January 23, 1978, issue, *there is an analysis of the very thing I mentioned regarding Mr. Graham's contribution to the local church.* According to that study, the local church is helped very little by the Graham crusades. I couldn't believe my eyes. Professional, scientific efforts were made to produce that report. I had only my shoebox and my grassroots eyes, but I knew what I was seeing. I've been to the Benton County Fair and seen a few things along the way. I deeply resent the way these superstars are held up as being great contributors to local churches, while those who play guard and tackle in the front line are put down or ignored. The paradox is that much of the personality's money comes from local church people, who honestly overestimate the spiritual returns.

Now I want to mention a good name. That name is Charles Allen. Charles Allen is pastor of the largest United Methodist church in the world. His church is a large church, but not one built on gimmicks like bussing. They telecast, but in no way can the church be called an Electric church. I love Charles Allen, and he knows it. We are friends—good friends. In my judgment, he is the best preacher in the world. I can't understand ministers who are envious of pastors like Charles. If in reading this you have thought my heart envious, you have missed my point.

The reason Charles Allen is in Houston, and I am not, is that I couldn't handle it. I know that. The same is true for the big names in Memphis or Little Rock or Nashville or Chicago. Those ministers are where they are because they deserve to be! I know there may be exceptions (and each preacher reading this can think of at least one), but on the whole, those are extraordinary people.

You are where you are, preacher friend, because that is where you are supposed to be. If that is not true, you have a problem bigger than your position—you have a theological problem. If you ought to be in Houston, then the God of this entire business has absented himself. If you believe that, you aren't a Theist (a believer in a present, powerful God)—you are a Deist (a believer in a God who is not involved). I'm not a Deist and neither should you be. You can't say the Lord's Prayer if you are.

76

Now and then I hear some young pastor say, "If I were in those places, I would put out more effort." If that is your sentiment, you'd better turn in your credit cards, for you will *never* be productive. I know the very idea that all of us are where we belong makes many of us say, "True, with one exception—me!" Nevertheless, I think this includes 99 percent of us. The pastor in Gravel Town can't hack it in Forrest City, and that is why he is where he is. I can't cut it at Marble Collegiate, and that is why I am here. The same goes for the rest of our ambitious brothers and sisters.

I have followed four rules for happiness in my churches. At first, my ambition led me to neurosis and an unproductive frame of mind. Then I had help from wiser heads. Let me share this help.

First, accept your people for what they are. They can't be like the people in the church you just moved from, so don't try to make them over. Never talk about how good it was where you were. They may pack your bags and rent a U-Haul. Finding one of those trucks in front of the parsonage would be disconcerting. The less you say about where you were, the better it will be for everyone.

Tell your people the things you like about their town and church—the plus side. *After* you do this, you will find them more receptive to your desire to correct the minus side. Many states are like Arkansas in one respect. One side of our state is influenced by more conservative customs; we call that "the hills." The other side of our state is "the flatland." Some of our preachers can negotiate both. But some of us try to force one mentality on the other. It will not work. People have to be loved where they are, and for what they are.

Second, let your people help you fight your battles. If you are right, you are not alone in anything you do. Once there was a woman in my congregation who didn't like anything I did. (I'll bet you've got one, too.) While the rest of the people were trying to forget a former pastor back down the line, she impressed upon all his successors that *he* was the only good pastor she ever had. During my first year, I had truly grown to love some of our little old ladies, and I made it a point to tell them so. There was a Sunday school class for

QUIT SAYING YOU ARE GOING TO STAY

this age group (70 and up). One day, the lady who couldn't stand me made a typically cutting remark in that class.

The word spread to my office between Sunday school and church services that three of my friends tore into her like lions that hadn't eaten in a month. They had that old gal for brunch! They would have done the same for my predecessor (because she slandered *him*, too), but he had never told them he loved them. So, he fought his battles alone.

When I stood for the call to worship I spotted her. She looked like she had been through a carwash without a car! I'll let you in on a secret. I savored the victory, even though my sword was never unsheathed. (If my ethics professor is still alive and reading this—forget it, Prof. I long ago fell from grace, because I enjoy thinking about it to this day.) From that day until I left, that woman never again as much as opened her mouth about me. Why, I wouldn't have given King Herod a dog's chance against my little old ladies.

Third, don't succumb to the delusion that you are bigger than your present position. If you do, you will never speak to your people where they are. During a period in my student days, some of us young preachers went out to country churches to preach revivals. These were the B-12 days for the local folks. We didn't have many sermons, and some of us used the same ones. When better sermons were published, we would preach them.

One sermon was titled, "Prepare to Meet Thy God." The theme was from the book of Amos, at the place where the great prophet calls Israel to repentance. In the published sermon, the preacher was supposed to call America to repentance. Several times during the sermon, the points were punctuated with, "Prepare to met thy God, O America!" Now that is heady wine. Imagine calling this entire country to her knees!

If you can't get the whole country's attention, you obviously have to improvise. So we did just that. We would address the town where we were speaking with the words of wrath.

One of my friends was called upon to hold a revival in Moscow, Arkansas. Now, Moscow is fifteen miles from Pine Bluff. Somehow the sins of Moscow didn't seem important enough for all the effort

needed to bring that town to its knees. But my friend improvised beautifully. He thundered out, "Prepare to meet thy God, O Pine Bluff!" Now, he was loud, but not loud enough to be heard for fifteen miles!

It didn't diminish his powerful presentation one bit to know he was purposefully overshouting Moscow. In fact, without benefit of the Pine Bluff City Council, he had annexed Moscow and enlarged the city limits. There is no way to be effective, if you think you are more important than those you are called to serve.

Fourth, have a sense of humor. No one ever told me this in my years of formal preparation. But I know it is true. It is very easy to take yourself too seriously. Your church has room for only one God. There will be times when a sense of humor is better for your mental state than a Davidic Psalm. That's not heresy! That's the gospel truth!

13

Wrestling Against Principalities and Powers and Walter Cronkite
(You Can't Beat Brinkley's Smirk, So Don't Try)

Do you know the greatest weakness in preaching? It is not length, loudness, or poor English. *It is lack of clarity.* That is our number-one sin against our congregations. I want to make an issue of this. I would like to shout it again and again. People don't know what we have said when we are finished.

A certain cliche has arisen during the past decade or so. It goes like this: "I heard him saying thus and so." Someone else will jump up and say, "Oh no, that is not what I heard him saying at all." On and on it goes. Finally we are forced to ask the one who started it all, "What *did* you say?"

Sometimes we have visiting bishops at our conference preaching events. A favorite post-sermon game is "What did you hear the bishop saying?" (We love our bishops, and we are grateful that some of them have great administrative ability.)

There is no excuse for lack of clarity. Yet, it is our most common fault. We might as well admit it. Sermons are cloudy for one of several reasons. Either we are not familiar with the subject, in which case we shouldn't have brought it up; we are fearful of putting into plain words what we really mean; or, we are poorly prepared. One of these three will usually nail our lazy hides to the wall.

I firmly believe people in all our churches will listen with open minds to most anything we say, if we will simply say it so they can understand it. We are boring our people to death, because we don't ever get to the point. Ralph Sockman used to say the best example of the term "loss of nerve" was the man who takes aim and can't pull the trigger.

Poorly prepared sermons are difficult to preach and difficult to listen to. Their logic has a tendency to break down. It cannot be braced up by authoritative quotations. There is nothing profound about a muddy sermon, even though you quote Paul Tillich till the cows come home. One of the best things you can do for your people is to preach your sermon so that they can quote back the main points.

We might as well face it. People are conditioned by television like Pavlov's dog to its bell. Walter Cronkite says it in a way they can understand, and *he* is talking about great issues. There is no excuse for the way some of us address our smalltown congregations. We are so wordy that if we were called upon to point some one quickly to the restroom, they might not make it in time.

Here are some suggestions:

First, start on Monday morning with your criticism of last Sunday's sermon. Also, *begin your preparation for next Sunday.* If you wait until Thursday or Friday to critique your past sermon, it will look like a masterpiece. The further away you are from the town garbage dump, the better it smells. If the sermon breaks down, note down the weaknesses as soon as you can. Don't file it away, only to repeat the same mistakes the next time you use it.

Many take Monday off. I have found this to be a mistake. Get a jump on the week by getting ahead of it. If you wait until the latter part of the week, you will surely have a funeral or hospital calls or even personal sickness. I had a friend who suffered from migraine headaches Friday and Saturday. I advised that he get his sermon done by Wednesday, so he could take Friday and Saturday in a more relaxed fashion. Later he wrote me that he was free as a bird when the countdown reached Sunday—because he was prepared.

Second, write down every word. Now, I know there is a lot of controversy on this point. But all those television commentators who speak to our people have every word written. They know exactly what they are going to say. Why shouldn't you? I don't intend for you to become slaves to your manuscripts. No, not at all. I am saying you can't help but know your subject, if you will write out what you mean to say.

This is the hardest job in the ministry. *Every* week, without fail, every preacher has to fight the temptation to write three or four main sentences, throw in a story, and then freewheel it. I can assure you that *your attendance percentage will pick up* if your people know you are working hard to meet parish needs. We might as well say it right here. The main reason we have poor preaching is because of pure laziness in preparation. Good preaching is seldom a gift. It is more often a result of disciplined study.

I never knew a single good preacher who was in trouble in his church. Now get this. I think it is possible for everyone who preaches to get better and better. That is accomplished by plain hard work. We can all improve and become relatively good preachers, if we will work harder at clarity. If something doesn't hold together or make sense to you when you write it, it will not clear up or get any more profound by leaving it in your notes until Sunday.

I am indebted for this advice to that preacher of preachers, Ralph Sockman. He spent five days in Malvern, Arkansas, in 1966. He was nearing eighty, and I was in my midthirties. I spent every minute I could with him. I asked him to teach me to preach. I noticed that when he preached, *every word* seemed to fit. I asked him if this was the result of a fine vocabulary. He grinned like a grandfather who had a toy for his grandchild and said, "Johnson, I'll tell *you* the secret. I have it memorized! I don't trust my vocabulary or my tendency to ramble."

I had him look at several of my sermons. He would say, "I see where you took off and chased rabbits here," or "What in the name of heaven did you mean here?" Now and then he would say, "You became tired here and decided to improvise on the spot, didn't you?"

I was naked before that man. He knew me as well as I knew myself. Then he said a most profound thing: "There is no such thing as great preaching without tiring work. Fosdick [Harry Emerson] used to tell me that he was exhausted after preparing a sermon.

"If you want to be a good preacher, you will be one of a minority of less than 10 percent. That is the percentage of people who, every single week, pay the price. Most start out with good intentions, but the price is too great." Then looking around and pointing out the window, he said, "There is not a single preacher in any of the small towns around here who could not hold his little congregation in rapt attention, if he paid the price of writing every word clearly and carefully."

He warned me about the insidious arguments against this kind of work. I asked if I would not be glued to my manuscript, and he said, "Only if you are not familiar with it." He remarked that I could reword it as I spoke, but that would still be better than creating the sentences on the spot.

We had breakfast every morning at seven o'clock in the restaurant adjacent to his motel room. One morning he was late, and I went to his room to inquire if something was wrong. He opened the door and asked me to come in. He was about half-shaved. Dr. Sockman wore old-fashioned suspenders, and one was off his right shoulder, so he could shave freely. Papers were all over a table and neatly stacked on the floor.

I asked what all that work meant. The old man said he was to preach at the Easter sunrise service at the Hollywood Bowl. Easter was a month or so away. He said he was running late for breakfast, because he had not gotten to bed until three o'clock that morning. He had spent all that time working on *one page!* I suggested that surely, as many times as he had preached on the resurrection, he must have suitable sermons in his barrel.

I'll never forget his reply: "Johnson, I want to speak on our Lord's resurrection with the thoughts and words of my life *now,* not something I prepared ten years ago. I may use the same words, but I want to be as fresh as I can."

He became an authority figure for me. I treasure at least fifteen letters I received from him. He never encouraged me to be great, but he always encouraged me to be the best preacher I could possibly be, at each stage of my life. I heard about his death soon after it happened. There was only one thing to do at that time, and that was to weep. A giant oak had fallen.

Third, be brief. Television people know that they can't hold our attention for more than ten minutes at a time, and they are the greatest in the world at communication. What makes you think

85

you can hold your congregation without a break for thirty minutes?

I truly believe a ten-to-fifteen-minute sermon with *every word clearly stated* will enhance your preaching effectiveness. I can illustrate it this way. Nearly all sermons have only ten minutes of material, at the most. All the remainder is padding. One day I checked a pastor's broadcast sermon tape. He wasted time and words in several different ways. There were thirty-one "you knows," seventy-seven "uhs" and "ands," and twelve outright repeated statements. In addition, he restated seven entire sections, using different words. Finally, he closed his sermon three times.

There weren't even ten minutes of real material in that sermon. Most of the time was wasted as he shifted gears, or found his place after losing it. And that was the pastor of a very large city church. If he can be guilty, what about the rest of us? We are competing against the greatest—not only famous preachers, but those marvelously well-trained newspeople on the tube!

14

Who Said Sameness Has to Be Dull?

Because we live in a world that is always changing, we are led to believe that sameness is bound to be dull. Changing fashions in clothing, cars, houses, furniture, life-styles, foods—all these and more, dictate that standing still is "death."

This theory has influenced our local churches. It has crept up on us like a slowly moving fog. Before we know it, we are rearranging the chancel furniture and turning up the spots. Religious television programs have all but abandoned pulpits, choir robes, and other traditional symbols. If some of our people on the local scene were to voice complaints about reciting the Apostles' Creed or the Lord's Prayer, or gripe about Holy Communion, away those things would go too!

Much has been written about the disappearance of tradition, and I will not labor the point. I do want to give fellow pastors of my vintage some suggestions about change.

Always remember, the *highs will kill you quicker than the lows*. Low blood pressure may make you a little sleepy, but high blood pressure will blow the lid off! Don't jump from one fad to the next. Planning a "shot in the arm" retreat every three months is deadly. Also, having in a guest superstar for periodic testimonies is no good. If we need one thing in our rapidly changing world, it is to be able to rely on something stable.

If you have to pump up your people on lay witness movements, weekend revivals and such, some of them will become dependent on those highs. They will become addicted. Before long, the highs will be looked upon as normal. When this happens, you will have divided your congregation. Many of the people don't want these injections into their blood stream. Their lives are so full of events

running from excessive highs to debilitating lows, that they can't handle any more. They surely don't need it in church. There will always be compulsive, frenetic people in every congregation. They are well-meaning and sincere. However, if you listen to them and set your church tempo to their pulse beat, you haven't learned much about human nature. The church service should always include sights, sounds, and methods which have proven themselves through the years. People want to feel they have been to church.

I can illustrate this with a beautiful story from David O. Woodyard's book, *Strangers and Exiles* (Westminster Press).

> One day this summer I found at our front door a three-year-old boy rubbing his eyes and sobbing gently. I asked him who he was and where he lived. The only thing he could communicate was his name, Tony. He pointed to his feet, which were bleeding from the stone roads. I picked him up and held him in my arms. After a few minutes I asked, "Tony, how are we going to find your home?" With renewed confidence and remarkable courage he looked at me and said, "You just start walking and I'll tell you when we get there."

The little boy knew he would recognize the security of his home because of the familiar and dependable things he would see. I always knew I was home when I walked into our house. There were smells and sounds that made me feel secure. Church is like these good odors from our mothers' kitchens. There always needs to be the element of dependability. If your church is a three-ring circus with new acts each week, you will lose your more stable people. I guarantee that!

Recently a friend sent me a large advertisement from his local paper. The event advertised was called "A Great Gittin' Up Day." A certain church was trying to reach a goal of 1,000 people. If they succeeded, the pastor would preach from the Coca Cola hot-air balloon. Second, a ten-speed bike was to be given to the boy or girl bringing in the most people. Third, the occupants of the church buses reaching their goals would see their respective drivers dunked in a tank of water. (I wondered if this meant they would be dunked in the baptistry.) Fourth, balloons and snow cones were to be given

89

to all, and a promise of a church dinner for everyone was made. With churches offering this kind of program for excitement, one wonders what the benefits of grace might be if the goal were 2,000. So much for an illustration of effective evangelism.

Second, don't make the people compete with each other over the degree of their righteousness. One way to make them compete is always to be beating some drum. People will soon tire of efforts to align them with the latest "priority."

Another sure way to divide them is to have bragging sessions during the announcement period. Someone will always be left out. We have an eleventh commandment in our church: "Thou shalt not announce!"

Think for a minute about the folly of the typical announcement. Suppose a Sunday school class wants you to announce a social. There are one hundred people in your congregation. That class has seven members. This means that ninety-three percent of the people hearing that announcement couldn't care less if that class had an ice cream party or a love-in. You will bore them to death. Now, compound this with a string of other announcements, each dealing with the activities of a small group, and you will waste five to ten minutes of valuable time. One good rule of thumb is never to make an announcement which does not involve the congregation as a *whole!*

There are so many insidious traps we fall into which encourage our people to compete. Everyday life is one great competitive event. Church should let up on them at this point. Services should be more reflective and less aggressive and agitating. There is nothing more annoying than to attend a worship service where the pastor brings in some outside speaker, and following the message, an offering is whipped up for his or her cause. Just as aggravating, is for the pastor to demand some kind of public response at the altar. Some pastors think of the most devious ways to get a public response. When a generation of preachers has passed through the life of a small congregation, just think how many times these same folks have had to demonstrate.

Also, watch the tendency to make hay at the expense of your neighboring pastor. Much is said about the ethics of visiting another's membership. I'll pass over that. What I want to bring up is something I have not seen challenged. Probably the most un-Christian page in the newspaper on Saturday is not the movie page. *It is the church page.* Notice the way one church cuts another to pieces. Take a good look at the ads. Insidious slogans run wild as each church vies for the attention of the reader. One such slogan is, "The Church Where the Visitor Is Never a Stranger!" This infers that all the other nearby churches will freeze you to death with their lack of concern. Or, "The Church Where the Old-fashioned Gospel Is Preached." This fellow is saying that the church down the street has a "new" gospel which is sure to fail you. Then there is "The Church Which Offers Life." Does this mean that corpses fill the mausoleum down the street?

One grand gesture of Christian kindness would be to cut that stuff out of our bulletins, and erase those silly slogans from our letterheads. When you have an ad in the paper, state the case without a competitive slap at your brothers or sisters. It's inexcusable for us to advertise as the breakfast food people do—or worse.

Third, in all your worship services, emphasize true priorities. Although I mentioned this earlier, I would like to list them here. The priorities people have now are the same ones our Lord saw when he was among us. They are:

1. the hunger of the human heart for reconciliation with God and humans
2. the enigma of the suffering of the innocent
3. the unrelenting trauma of death

Every service should focus in some way on these priorities. I don't ever focus on any other. Through literature and group meetings, we can cover other things. I never promote the latest cause of my denomination from the pulpit. We *support* these causes, but they are not our true priorities. There is a difference between a cause and a priority. Be prepared to do more at eleven o'clock than raise money.

These special interests are a sanctified lobby! There is no other way to describe them. Pastors are forced into the role of "cause master," and the typical congregation is too often treated as a "cornered" audience. Before these cornered people pass one special-offering plea after another. The fact that they are all for good causes is not relevant to the issue. Our people have only so much money to give.

I would propose that there be some kind of moratorium on special offerings, other than for unforeseen crises, such as tornado relief, and such. Congregations should be spared the endless cause efforts and special-offering emphases that are strung out all year long. All these causes should be limited to once-a-year appeals. We could do it in a business-like way, through a United Fund–type gift, rather than picking the congregation's pockets two or three times a month. The local churches could include or exclude them at budget time. The argument that we need to sensitize people to these needs is greatly overstated. The plain truth is that *we have made people numb!*

There is yet another bad effect of special offerings during the service. They further divide the congregation. Each one of these causes has a representative voice within the congregation. This affords a perfect setting for something I have seen and despised during my entire pastoral life. Special appeals give individuals the opportunity to make sizeable (and usually very public) contributions to particular causes. The same giver may not give very much to the overall budget. I have praticed and preached that one should tithe the bulk of what one gives to the total budget in an unrestricted manner. I think the majority of my parishers have done this. It becomes galling when some soul who gives, for example, $300 per year, stands up and leads some cause with a pledge of $100. This makes the person who may give $2,000 to the annual budget, with no strings attached (and no accolades), look as if he does not care as much for the "special" need as the person who starts the ante! Small churches are wracked with such situations. If we published open accounts of undesignated and designated giving, not only would it shock our people, it would stop this hypocritical activity overnight!

I have discovered that the best way to raise money for these denominational causes is *not to talk about them so much.* If the local church ministers to the basic priorities I mentioned earlier, it will create a receptive environment for worthy denominational causes. When people's souls are helped, you can depend on them to come to the aid of your causes. For example, our church decided to have women as trustees and in other important positions. We did just that without one word from the pulpit or banner in the hall. People are tired of the endless crusades. I believe that with all my heart. Sometimes these passing, transient emphases are called *priorities*. This is wrong. The priorities of the human dilemma were articulated even before the day of Jesus. They never change! Emphases change, priorities do not. If the local church will concentrate on the true *priorities*, there will be plenty of money for the changing *emphases*.

A mother once said to me, "Does God have anything to say to a mother whose child has cancer?" I was glad to see her, because she had been by her child's side for months. Bruised and battered, she needed to come to worship service. I would have failed her, if she could not have taken home with her some word that met her need. Pastor, your church, regardless of size, has people with needs like that. Don't fail your people by emphasizing superficial causes!

Here is another thought. *Sing some happy songs.* I don't want to get into a war with music people. I do not want to debate which hymn is good or bad. I only know that some of the hymns, though worded well, are terrible to have to sing. I know why our people like gospel songs. It is because they are happy songs. This life is morbid enough without dirge-like music on Sunday. " 'Tis So Sweet to Trust in Jesus" may not be acceptable at Sunday morning worship in some churches, but it's their loss. And it's not a bad idea!

My last suggestion is simple. *Who says you have to meet for an hour?* I have a policy based on the observation of many years, and on my visits to other churches. Your people will not be receptive to your sermon if you have kept them for much more than twenty minutes before you begin. Those drawn-out periods of thirty to thirty-five minutes will have them worn out before you stand up to preach. The choir works hard with me at this point. I place great emphasis on ritual, but it must not be tedious or poorly planned.

We are often boring our people with lengthy readings of Scripture. I am familiar with the arguments regarding the

Christian year and lectionary emphases. I follow the *general* emphasis, but I am not a slave to it. A five-minute reading of passages is *too long. I read only that portion of the Bible I have time to explain.* I don't think the Bible can walk on all fours. It requires explanation. It is better to read one verse and help the people digest it, than to read a whole chapter while they are leafing through the hymnal. Try this method. You may like it.

No ordinary service should last over forty-five or fifty minutes, at the most. The news of the world takes only thirty well-planned minutes. Why should we think that it takes an hour to amble through peoples' lives in Dew Point Springs, USA?

15

God Bless the Little Old Ladies Because My Wife Will Be One Someday!

We are all the recipients of help from institutions. And we are the people who constructed and created those institutions for our own well-being. This is a sure sign of a civilized society. I want us now, laity and ministers alike, to join hands and take a look at this old institution, the church.

I believe human beings have three basic needs. The local church can meet these needs, if it is happy and well adjusted. Meeting these needs has nothing to do with size. *Every* church can do it.

First, there is our need for friendship. That is why I've called this chapter "God Bless the Little Old Ladies." I am not joking about them, but rather pointing up the stability they represent. They symbolize much that is good in church life. Theirs is the truly stable economy our government is always wishing for.

That stability is what the local church is all about. It is the place we can find true and lasting friends. In one of Paul's rambling commentaries on his life, he makes a most poignant statement about a former friend and ally. In several previous references, Paul mentioned Demas and in Second Timothy 4:10, he says, "Demas hath forsaken me, having loved this present world."

I don't know much about Demas, but I do know he didn't know where true friendship lay. Of all the words our Lord could have used to address Judas in Gethsemane, Jesus called him, "Friend." Judas had sinned against friendship.

The fact that my parishioners are my friends is worth more than words can describe. Living among them in their joys and sorrows is most rewarding. A couple of years ago I was at a wedding reception when a lady from another town bent her head over my glass and inquired if this were not champagne. I affirmed the sin. She then said that recently she had a wedding and their pastor (who was of

95

my denomination) had hurt them deeply by refusing to come to the reception because they served champagne. I knew one thing about that fellow. He didn't know the difference between a battle and the total war. He won his battle, but he lost the war!

I said, "Lady, I cry with my people in their sorrow, and I rejoice with them in their happiness." Pastor friend, you don't have to drink the champagne, but don't make a fool of yourself by refusing to attend the reception. The greatest preacher of all time went to a wedding reception in Galilee. *If your people are not your friends, it is doubtful if you are truly their pastor.*

Second, there is the human need for a sense of personal worth. This is what the gospel of Jesus Christ is all about. The gospel tells us that we are worth something. This is a tough world to get through. The older I get, the more questions arise in my mind regarding the complex human dilemma. One aspect of this complexity is that the vastness of it all makes individuals feel unimportant and worthless.

Failure threatens us at every turn. We live with it. We face it in our plans. We feel it in our bones. I think the woman who washed Jesus' feet with her tears was crying tears of joy for one big reason. He made her feel she was worth something. All those other fellows looked right through her. She was a public utility, and they weren't buying, at the time.

The local church is a spot where people can reaffirm their sense of personal worth. I hate to hear older people talk about being worn out and in the way. As long as we have breath, we must value ourselves and one another.

I never did like to regiment Sunday school classes for adults according to age. We have removed all age barriers in our adult division. A fantastic thing developed. We have young couples meeting with older couples. They are adding to one another's well-being. One gentleman in our church is seventy-nine. He refuses to go to the senior citizens' meeting when he knows it will be "ache and tell" time. He will be refreshing to be around right up to the day he stumbles dying off the eighteenth green. He says being around younger men has helped him keep a better perspective.

Our third human need is contact with a reality beyond ourselves. This

97

life is a pilgrimage. It is a journey. It is over all too soon. I really don't know where the past twenty-five years have gone. I share what all parents experience—we have our children with us one day, and the next they are gone. Life becomes a blur.

I see people every Sunday who share this pilgrimage with me. There may be a lot of other ways for people to experience ultimate reality, but the best way I know is in the Christian faith. People are crisscrossing this world, looking for mountains to climb, in the hope of finding a wise man at the top to point them to reality. That reality is at home in their local church!

Henry F. Lyte was an Anglican minister who suffered untold anguish in his life. He had personality difficulties with his parishioners that nearly drove him insane. He also suffered from a condition similar to asthma that took its toll in everything he did.

After he died, his relatives found the words to a poem, "Abide with Me." It was later set to music by W. H. Monk. Notice the words of the first and last stanzas:

> Abide with me; fast falls the eventide;
> The darkness deepens; Lord, with me abide!
> When other helpers fail and comforts flee,
> Help of the helpless, O abide with me.
>
> Hold thou thy cross before my closing eyes;
> Shine through the gloom and point me to the skies;
> Heaven's morning breaks, and earth's vain shadows flee;
> In life, in death, O Lord, abide with me.

The corner church has been a place where fellow travelers on this earthly pilgrimage can come together and hold the cross up before their eyes. Maybe some people can find a way to meet these three needs elsewhere. I won't argue that point. I do believe that though one, or maybe even two, may be met individually somewhere else, there is no place where all three are met year after year, day after day, as well as in the local church.

I consider it a challenge and a victory that our hometown churches can meet such basic universal human needs. Now that, in itself, is a reason for gratitude and joy.

16

The Church Has a Pretty Good Track Record with Kids

There are people who have doubts about the value of local churches. But not one of them is a child. When children pass puberty, they may begin to resist our insistence that they attend church, but from age one to twelve, I assure you, they love the church.

Children of that age don't have hangups about anything. A little boy may resent having a little sister, and a little girl may dislike having to live with a little brother, but that's about as far as their troubles extend. For the average child, church is a thing of delight. They love to go.

The church is not out-of-date to a child. That is a wonderful fact. Children never tire of wholesome routines. In fact, they come to place great dependence upon doing the same things over and over. Try changing a child's routine in something he holds dear, and he will tell you it should "go this way" or "that way". Children love to sing the Doxology and Gloria Patri. They love to quote the Lord's Prayer. Look at them sometime as they do it. They get lost in much of the service, but what they know, they do with gusto.

Also, children are not burdened down with judgments of others. They excuse human frailty. Older, more experienced sinners are sometimes down on the church because of the supposed hypocrites in the pews. Children are not so inclined. I suppose they can't tell which ones are hypocrites, so it doesn't bother them much.

The chairman of my board has a four-year-old son who has lived fully every day of his life. I think he may even have borrowed a day or two from someone else. He moves so fast it is difficult for him to keep everyone straight.

Not long ago my picture appeared in the local paper with a group of men. When the boy's mother saw it she said, "Jim, do you know who this is?"

He looked up and said, "I don't know his name, but he goes to our church." Now that is a humbling assessment, especially from one of the chairman's family. But it does serve to make a point. He might not have understood my role, but that kid had me as a member of "our church" firmly planted in his mind.

There is a little girl named Mary who, since she has been old enough to walk, has come and hugged me around the legs until I picked her up. But her grandfather almost ruined my postsermon hugs. Mary had thought I was God because of my white robe, until he informed her differently. Jim may underplay my role, and Mary may overplay it, but the church is batting a thousand with both of them.

Another thing we can learn from children is *their belief that God is real*. God is as real to a child as Jesus was to the people of his day. How marvelous that is. They can see God in *everything*. When they get as old as we are, they may have a hard time seeing God in *anything*. I think this aspect of childhood is what our Lord meant when he said "of such is the kingdom of heaven." Their imagination always seems to do the image of God a favor. We imagine the negative side of God. They see God as somehow getting good out of every situation. They can look past a car wreck and see a field where children are playing.

If people in local churches can learn anything from children, it is that God is close by. They believe he is as hurt as we are over a bad situation. He may not be as confused as we are, but he *is* acquainted with our tears. My favorite account of God's involvement with a child is the story of the mother who was listening as her litle girl described the elephant in the backyard.

After a description that would put a tour guide to shame, the mother said, "Show me the elephant." The little girl showed her a big charred stump. In amusement, the mother said, "You know that is not an elephant. Look here, feel it, touch it. It is a stump. What gave you the idea it was an elephant?"

The child promptly answered, "God told me." To this the

shocked mother demanded that she go to her room and tell God she was sorry that she had told an untruth about him. After a time had passed, the little girl came out beaming with a great big smile.

"Well, what did God say about your story?" asked the mother.

The child answered, "He said that was okay; the first time he saw it, he thought it was an elephant, too!"

When God is real to us, we learn that he is near, near enough so that we, like Moses, can speak to him as one speaks to a friend.

The third thing we can learn from children is that *they get right down to the basics.* Children get this from the local church. When I think of basics, I think of the hours I have seen men and women spend in Sunday school rooms with the children. Only God himself knows the infinite value of having children in a church, learning about his word.

I am always indebted to collectors of stories about children. *Pulpit Digest* has, on occasion, run across some of the best. On the subject of getting down to the basics, I have gleaned two from them over the years.

Once a mother asked her five-year-old to say grace at the table, when guests were present. The little boy was frightened at this request. Wanting to show the little fellow off, the mother said, "Son, you can just say what you have heard mother say."

At this the little boy bowed his head and said, "Dear God, why did I invite these people here on such a hot day?"

The second story is of the four-year-old who was spending the night away from home. At bedtime, expecting the usual prompting, she knelt at her hostess' knee to say her prayers. Finding her hostess unable to help her, she prayed: "Please, God, 'scuse me. I can't remember my prayers and I'm staying with a lady who doesn't know any."

Getting down to the basics. Kids believe the local church is where the basics are taught! Don't tell them any different, my friend. They will not believe you. We've always done well with kids!

17

The Local Church Is Not Yet Ready for the Obituary Section

I want to make three hopeful observations about the revival of the local church. It is time to stop wording her obituary. Around the corner I see a new day. I may be too optimistic, but that's my mood. Lou Holtz, the Arkansas Razorback football coach, is famous for his one-liners. He says that "the light at the end of the tunnel could be an oncoming train." In this case, I sincerely hope not.

First, I predict the return of the local church's importance. There is a nostalgic feeling in this country at the present time, and we will soon see evidence of it in the local church. In fact, there is much evidence now. It is part of the return to smaller things. "Think small" is a motto that is saying it more and more for many of us.

There was a time when young ministerial aspirants dreaded the small local church. It is not so now. More and more of these young people are looking forward to life in small towns. The local church is seen as basic to the Christian mission. And society's tendency to treat people as numbers has enhanced the intimate and personal image of the local church.

Second, I predict a reaction against the religious media mania. We all recall some of the experiences television has had in expanding good thirty-minute programs into sixty minutes. Many excellent thirty-minute programs were over-exposed when they expanded. They paid a severe price. The same will be true for television religious stars. There are so many now it is difficult to keep track of them. Everyone is doing something different for Jesus. I read recently of a "stripper for Jesus," and it was not someone who removes paint.

Third, I predict a greater emphasis on meditation and prayer. Religion

today is loud and noisy. It is on the level of entertainment, and many of us despise this trend. I can remember when we didn't clap in church. The media personalities encourage applause for each performance. Time on the tube is so costly, those fellows can't afford to be quiet. You never see moments for meditation on those programs. They are too busy controlling our every thought. They dare not give us time for reflection on what they have just said or done. The local chuch has time for quietness, adoration, meditation, and all those necessary elements of the Christian religion. We will soon come out of the frenzy brought on by efforts to get us to be more emotional in our worship. If folks want to wave their hands, that's all right with me. It is nothing new, however!

Twenty years ago this past fall, my wife and I were invited to a church of that temperament. The pastor was a good friend, a good man, and a sincere person. He wanted us to attend a revival. Was it ever a revival! The pastor and his evangelist sat on the platform while the song leader did his thing. I spotted my friend waving his hand in my direction. I thought he was waving at me. Every five minutes or so he would wave in my direction. At first I just nodded an "I see you, brother" nod. Presently, the evangelist began to wave. Well, I knew he didn't know me, so I thought someone behind me was the focus of attention.

When the pastor finally explained his waving, he said he was doing so for the benefit of the visitors. *He had been waving at Jesus.* In fact, both of those fellows up there had been waving at Jesus! Everyone but me seemed to know what they were doing. I guess he decided to explain because he got tired of my returning his wave. If he could have located Jesus on the other side of the house, he might have saved us both a lot of trouble.

Now, that was all right for him and for those people, but I have trouble relating to it, hard as I try.

The local church is about the only place left in our society where one can find quiet and peace. The prelude should never be looked upon as music to chat by. I am finding that more and more of our young couples are thoughtfully reading the words of the hymns. Our come-and-go communion on Christmas Eve finds large groups of people sitting in the majesty of solitude. They seem to love it. It answers a need they can't fill elsewhere.

Yes, the local church has something good in store for itself—a better sense of appreciation. I'm glad we have local chuches where people can meditate, or wave at Jesus. Aren't you?

18

If Rex Doesn't Preach
Your Funeral,
Who Will?

When we talk about value received for money spent, the local church is on top all the way. It is impossible to list all the values people receive from small local churches. This has been done in other books and by more skillful writers, so I won't try. I have tried to offer hints and suggestions. I have tried to give hope to all of us who love the churches that dot our countryside and small towns. I have not tried to justify or defend the small church. I am writing for people who are beyond that stage.

The point of this book is that all of us can be happier in our work. I have found that the best way to be happy with something is to appreciate it at the *point of utility*. Just what is its utilitarian value in my life? I want to offer three ideas. No organization can surpass the local church at doing the things that matter most. Rex Humbard may thrill you, but he can't hold your hand!

The church is with us every day of our lives. We pass by churches on every trip we take. We see them so often that we look right through them. Recently, our church leased a large orange light that comes on at night. It lights up the entire church building with a glow of warmth. This building stands on a busy highway like a symbol. There is hardly a road we will ever travel that does not have some church close by.

I know the arguments as to why one doesn't have to belong to a church. Those are good on the surface. I have heard them all my life. I also know that a building can't save my soul. Nevertheless, it is a fact that the central position of the many church buildings in our towns symbolizes something of the power of the church in our

lives. That is why the early colonists built their houses around the church building.

I remember well a beautiful experience a long time ago. I was to go with a pastor to a home for the evening meal, during a summer revival. The pastor told me that we had to go several miles down a logging road, which became almost impassable when it rained. The house was located about a quarter of a mile from a river. In that home were five children and their father. The mother had died several years before.

The table was adorned with fresh-picked spring flowers. A chair was at either end, and benches were placed at the sides of the table. Fresh catfish, pinto beans, potatoes, and, of course, corn bread were in abundance. The children were scrubbed clean. Their manners were impeccable. An eight-year-old girl was the youngest, and a twenty-four-year-old young woman was the oldest. Three others were in between.

The story is really about the oldest and the youngest. The oldest girl was not beautiful, but she was attractive and winsome. I asked her father, when he and I were alone, why she didn't marry. He told me that the girl had promised her mother that before she left home, she would see the baby girl through her twelfth year. The mother had said that she was leaving the children to the care of the father, the oldest daughter, and the church. This didn't mean that they were wards of the church. The church had not had to give them any material help.

The mother intended that those children hear from her deathbed where real security lay. Though that home was as far as it could be from material things, the church had made its impact. I later discovered that many times the oldest girl had carried the little ones over stretches of high water to meet the schoolbus two miles away. The father had to be at work at daybreak, consequently he had to use his truck. This left the loving older sister to see four children through uncommon conditions, whenever they left that wilderness.

I asked if I could come back for another meal, and the family was delighted. I requested the same food again, because it was delicious and plentiful. On my second visit, the man made this statement:

"Brother Johnson, before I joined the church, I made it awful hard on my wife and family. The church has really made a lot of difference in our home."

I learned many lessons from that family. There was a selfless girl who could have dated every night; instead, she went out no more than once a month. I saw a home where the church made a lot of difference.

Second, the church is with us in our suffering. Christ left us a legacy to care for hurting people. People truly suffer in this life. When we are young, suffering seems something of an illusion. The older we get, the more of it we see. As I look out over my congregation, I know there are people present who are hurting deep within. I'm glad they have an environment like our church to help them.

Christ taught us to look into the human heart. When we do, it gives us compassion for all mankind. We are all probing why we were born. We are trying to make some sense out of this life. I had sung "Rescue the Perishing" for years, and never truly paid much attention to the third stanza. We always had a habit of leaving the third stanza out. But recently I noticed these words:

> Down in the human heart,
> Crushed by the tempter,
> Feelings lie buried that grace can restore;
> Touched by a loving heart,
> Wakened by kindness,
> Chords that were broken will vibrate once more.

The local church is the place where broken chords learn to vibrate once more. The anguish of suffering is a sobering reality.

The third basic reason I am grateful to be a part of the local church is that it is a haven in death. If I have heard this once, I have heard it too may times to count: "If it were not for our church, I couldn't have made it." Death is the final enemy. I have lived long enough to realize how powerful a foe it is. We are never ready for it. At this point I could resort to preaching about death's power. I shall refrain. The church is a place of refuge in death.

This past spring I visited our hospital late one Thursday night. The hospital administrator was also doing late business. To say that we admired each other is putting it mildly. I loved him for the work he did and his manner of doing it. He cared for people as few men I have ever known.

Each Sunday, unless he was called to the hospital, he was in the second pew with his family. As we were talking in the corridor, I remarked that I had heard him sing every note of Sunday's closing hymn, "Come, Thou Fount." He said he knew every word by heart because he had sung that song all his life.

He was an upbeat kind of guy, a young forty-one, always making people cheerful. I told him of one of my congregation who was in critical condition, and how seeing so much suffering sometimes depressed me. He said the same was true in his business. Then, just as I was saying goodby, he said with a smile, "Man, don't kid me about singing too loud in church. Sometimes *all you have in this life is a song.*"

I was called at nine-thirty Saturday night and told that he had died of a massive coronary. I cannot express in words the sudden anguish of my heart. He left a wife, a high school boy, and a grade school daughter. As I drove to the house, my soul cried out unspeakably. There were the whys and all the rest. Life didn't make sense. It all too often doesn't. About all I had was a faith I really couldn't feel, because of grief. But, I was the family's pastor, and I had a job to do.

Walking up the driveway, I realized that a tune was running through my head, "Come, Thou Fount of Every Blessing." That cryptic phrase jumped out at me:

> Here I raise mine Ebenezer;
> Hither by thy help I'm come;
> And I hope, by thy good pleasure,
> Safely to arrive at home.

I remembered enough Hebrew to recall that Ebenezer was an idiom for "help." An Ebenezer was a symbol of hope. My friend had said, "Sometimes all you have in this life is a song." All we have is an Ebenezer. I was sure he had arrived safely at home. There were more people at his funeral than in the entire town where I served my first church.

That is not the end of the story. When Christmas came around, the young person who came to my office to ask about the Christmas wreaths the youth group was selling was Gene's twelfth-grade son. Gene's wife was busy at the task of coordinating our elementary church school work, and his fifth-grade daughter took her place at the chancel as an acolyte. This family is firmly tied to our church.

The local church makes a difference in our everyday lives, in our encounters with suffering, and in our final battles with death. *There is no other representation of the Christian faith that can do these things as well.*